BHAJAN SWARLIPI

Part-4

Famous Bhajans and Sargam

Notations Writer: Vinod Kumar

Notion Press

NOTION PRESS

India. Singapore. Malaysia.

ISBN xxx-x-xxxxx-xx-x

DEDICATION

This book is dedicated to my Parents.

-Vinod Kumar

CONTENTS

PRAY GOD

JAI RADHE SHYAM

This life is four days fair. Do not waste it. You have got this human body fortunately. Make it better by singing Bhajan and Praying God. Life is rushing and always busy. At the end of this life, nothing will go with you. Only your prayers and bhajan will take you across this life's ocean. With the help of this book, play and sing bhajans and get Moksh at the feet of GOD.

Jay Radhe Krishna.

-VINOD KUMAR

Vinod Kumar

PREFACE

My hearty greetings and Namaste to Readers. I have written 51 Songs' Sargam books of Mukesh-1,2, Kishor-1,2, Lata, Asha, Manna dey, Yesudas, Kumar Shanu, Rafi-1,2,3,4, and SD Burman's composed song book in Hindi Language and translated many books in English SARGAM and Western CDEFG. Bhajan Swarlipi 1,2,3 and one Gazal Sargam book is also published in Hindi, English and Western notes. All these books are available online. Now Bhajan Swarlipi, Part-4 is available. It is in English with notes in SRGM style, so that music lovers can play and sing songs and get enjoyed. A person having basic knowledge of music can play the songs on any instrument.

Mostly song's notations are written in original scale but somewhere you have to transpose +1 or − 1 or ±2 to get original scale. Sa taken is also mentioned in each song's detail. Person who knows western notations can understand as given below:

.नी	.नी	सा	रे॒	रे	ग॒	ग	म
.N̲	.N	S	R̲	R	G̲	G	M
.B^b	.B	C	D^b	D	E^b	E	F
.A$^\#$	.B	C	C$^\#$	D	D$^\#$	E	F

मे॒	प	ध॒	ध	नी॒	नी	सां	रें॒
M*	P	D̲	D	N̲	N	S′	R̲′
G^b	G	A^b	A	B^b	B	C′	D$^{b′}$
F$^\#$	G	G$^\#$	A	A$^\#$	B	C′	C$^{\#′}$

In this book some symbols are given as (G -) it means you have to play G for two beats duration or matra similarly you have to play for the beats for more number of –(dash), if there are more dashes. When two notes are written adjacending to each other it means you have to play the notes in one beat or matra as MP mapa is played in one beat.

Lower Octave notes are written a dot before them as .G .A .B^b .B
Middle Octave notes are written simple C D E F G A B
Higher Octave notes are written an appostrophy after it C' D' E' etc.

Notations at the beginning of the song are prelude and notations in the middle of the song are interlude. These notations are written by me by my experience. Hope readers shall understand, like and enjoy it.

One has to practice sargam daily and its palte also so that one can become expert in playing difficult notes sequence. People can enjoy your playing instruments and then only your success will be counted. Care has been taken to provide accuracy still there is no liability of correctness and accuracy of notes and writer, printer, publisher and editor is not respoinsible for any error or ommissions or mistakes. If any mistake is found kindly inform.

Please visit notionpress.com or flipkart.com or indiamart.com and amazon.in to purchase the books. Kindly review my books at amazon and flipkart and give proper stars after purchasing my books from the above sites. For any query, email to me.

- Vinod Kumar (vinod66vk@gmail.com)

Vinod Kumar

SARGAM

SARGAM swars/sound are derived from voice of animals and birds. C scale is as follows:-

Note Name	Swar	Swar name	Swar full name	Swar full name in Hindi	Swar is derived from the voice of Bird/Animal
C=	Sa=	सा	Shadaj	षडज	Peacock/ मोर की आवाज़
D=	Re=	रे	Rishabh	रिषभ	Papiha /पपीहा की आवाज़
E=	Ga=	ग	Gandhar	गन्धार	Goat/ बकरा की आवाज़
F=	Ma=	म	Madhyam	मध्यम	Crane/ बगुला की आवाज़
G=	Pa=	प	Pancham	पंचम	Koccoo/Koyal/ कोयल की आवाज़
A=	Dha=	ध	Dhaiwat	धैवत	Frog/ दादुर या मेंढक की आवाज़
B=	Ni=	नी	Nishad	निषाद	Elephant हाथी की आवाज़
C'=	Sa'=	सां	(Higher Sa)		

C#=$\underline{Re}$=रे (रे कोमल), D#=$\underline{Ga}$=ग (ग कोमल), F#=Ma*=मे (म तीव्र), G#=$\underline{Dha}$=ध (ध कोमल), A#=$\underline{Ni}$=नी (नी कोमल)

We can write as S $\underline{R}$ R $\underline{G}$ G M M* P $\underline{D}$ D $\underline{N}$ N S'

All notes underlined are called Komal Swar as Komal Re, Komal Ga, Komal Dha, Komal Ni. One note Ma* is called Tivra Ma. Learn this table to know sequence of the notes-

S	$\underline{R}$	R	$\underline{G}$	G	M	M*
सा	रे	रे	ग	ग	म	मे
C	D^b	D	E^b	E	F	G^b
C	$C^\#$	D	$D^\#$	E	F	$F^\#$

P	D̲	D	N̲	N	S'
प	ध̲	ध	नी̲	नी	सां
G	A^b	A	B^b	B	C'
G	G$^\#$	A	A$^\#$	B	C'

Sa and Pa are Shudha Swar they do not have any Komal or Tivra. They are fixed notes as per North Indian music tradition.

OCTAVE

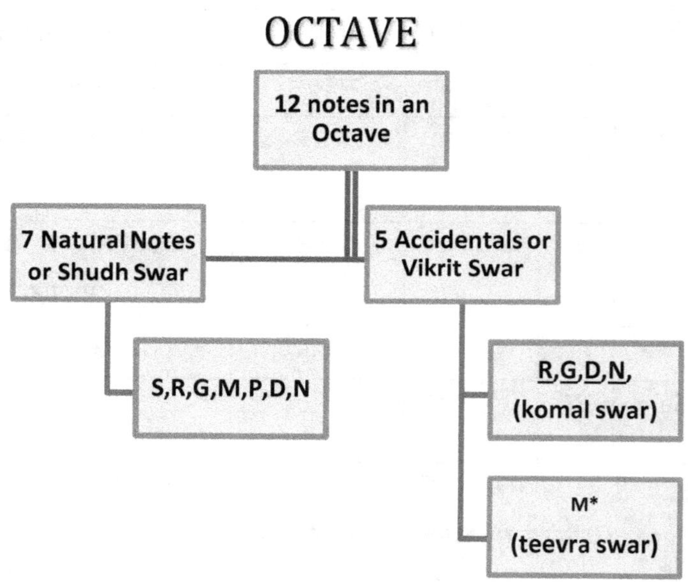

Sequence of the notes on any instrument are:

.D̲ .D .N̲ .N S R̲ R G̲ G M M* P D̲ D N̲ N S' R̲' R' G̲' G'

Vinod Kumar

C Scale is given as: SRGMPDNS′

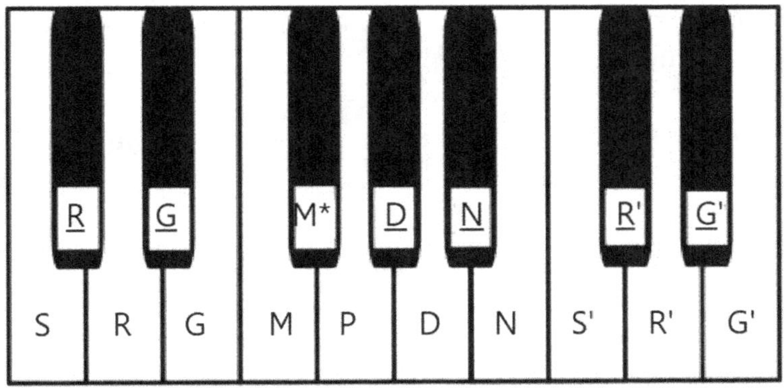

C# Scale is given as: SRGMPDNS′

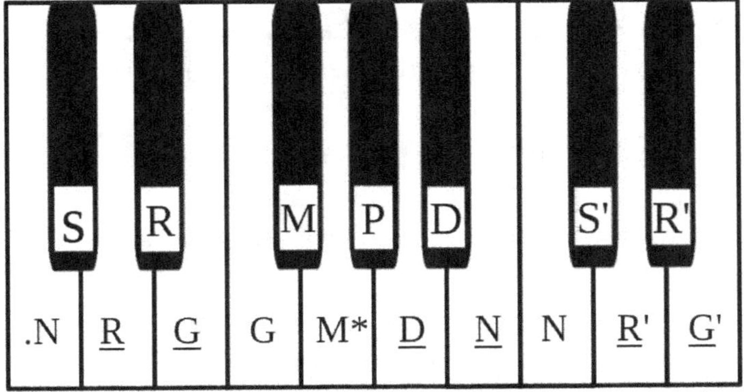

1. AJ MATHURA DE VICH AVTAAR

Krishna Bhajan   Singer: Nikunj Kaamra
Taal: Kaharwa fast   Chord: SGP   S=C#
https://youtu.be/VoOQxGiVopk

o aaj mathura de vich avtar ho gaya, shyam nikka jeya
shyam nikka jeya ho shyam nikka jeya

ho shyam chori chori jelaan vich jamya, ho jamya
ho naam sun ke sukhi sansar ho gaya, shyam nikka jeya

ho mata devki ne chhati naal la leya, ho la leya
vasudev ji ne tokri ch pa leya, han pa leya
mathura chhad ke gokul avtaar ho gaya, shyam nikka jeya

kitthe jamya te kitthe shyam palya, haan palya
charan chhu ke yamuna de paar ho gaya, shyam nikka jeya

saare devta ne ful barsaanvde, barsaanvde
naale geet khushi de gaanvde, haan gaanvde
baba nand de dware da singar ho gaya shyam nikka jeya

shyam rang utte kaale kaale vaal ne, haan vaal ne
osdi surat ton daas balihaar ho gaya shyam nikka jeya

Vinod Kumar

AJ MATHURA DE VICH AVTAAR

dhage 12	nti 34	nke 56	dhin 78	dhage 12	nti 34	nke 56	dhin 78	dhage 12	nti 34	nke 56	dhin 78	dhage 12	nti 34	nke 56	dhin 78
													S	S	S
													o	a	j
S	R	R	G	G	G	R	S	S	-R	R	-G	G	-	R	-S
m	thura	-	de	vi	ch	a	v	ta	-r	ho	-g	ya	-	shya	-m
R	S	S	S	-	P	P	-	P	D	P	M	G	R	R	G
nik	ka	je	ya	-	ho	shya	-m	nik	ka	je	ya	ho	-	shya	-m
R	R	S	S	-	S	S	S	S	R	R	G	G	G	R	S
nik	ka	je	ya	-	ho	a	j	m	thura	-	de	vi	ch	a	v
S	-R	R	-G	G	-	R	-S	R	S	S	S	-			
ta	-r	ho	-g	ya	-	shya	-m	nik	ka	je	ya	-			
													P	P	-
													ho	shya	-m
P	D	P	M	G	G	R	S	S	R	R	G	-	-	R	S
cho	ri	cho	ri	je	lan	vi	ch	j	m	ya	-	-	-	ha	-
R	S	S	-	-	S	S	-	S	R	R	G	G	-	R	S
j	m	ya	-	-	ho	na	-m	su	n	ke	su	khi	-	sn	-
S	-R	R	G	G	-	R	-S	R	S	S	S	-			
sa	-r	ho	g	ya	-	shya	-m	nik	ka	je	ya	-			
													P	P	P
													ho	ma	ta
P	D	P	M	G	G	R	-S	S	R	R	G	-	-	R	S
de	v	ki	ne	chha	ti	na	-l	la	le	ya	-	-	-	ha	-
R	S	S	-	-	P	P	P	P	-D	P	M	G	G	R	S
la	le	ya	-	-	ho	va	su	de	-v	ji	ne	to	k	ri	ch
S	R	R	G	-	-	R	S	R	S	S	-	-	-	S	S
pa	le	ya	-	-	-	ha	-	pa	le	ya	-	-	-	m	thura

S	R	R	G	G	G	R	S	S	-R	R	-G	G	-	R	-S
chh	d	ke	go	ku	l	a	v	ta	-r	ho	g	ya	-	shya	-m
R	S	S	S	-											
nik	ka	je	ya	-											

2. ANANT SANSAAR SAMUDRA TAAR

Guru Paduka Strot   Chord: SGP RMD   S=C#
Taal: Daadra
https://youtu.be/EYfLp_uOVgg

anantha samsara samudhra thara
naukayithabhyam guru bhakthithabhyam,
vairagya samrajyadha poojanabhyam,
namo nama sri guru padukhabyam. 1

kavithva varasini sagarabhyam,
dourbhagya davambudha malikabhyam,
dhoorikrutha namra vipathithabhyam,
namo nama sri guru padukhabyam. 2

natha yayo sripatitam samiyu
kadachidapyasu daridra varya,
mookascha vachaspathitham hi thabhyam,
namo nama sri guru padukhabyam. 3

naleeka neekasa pada hrithabhyam,
nana vimohadhi nivarikabyam,
nama janabheeshtathathi pradhabhyam
namo nama sri guru padukhabyam. 4

nrupali mouleebraja rathna kanthi
sariddha raja jjashakanyakabhyam,
nrupadvadhabhyam nathaloka pankhthe,
namo nama sri guru padukhabyam. 5

papandhakara arka paramparabhyam,
thapathryaheendra khageswarabhyam,
jadyadhi samsoshana vadaveebhyam
namo nama sri guru padukhabyam. 6

shamadhi shatka pradha vaibhavabhyam,
samadhi dhana vratha deeksithabhyam,
ramadhavadeegra sthirha bhakthidabhyam,
namo nama sri guru padukhabyam. 7

swarchaparana makhileshtathabhyam,
swaha sahayaksha durndarabhyam,
swanthachad bhava pradha poojanabhyam,
namo nama sri guru padukhabyam. 8

kaamadhi sarpa vraja garudabhyam,
viveka vairagya nidhi pradhabhyam,
bhodha pradhabhyam drutha mokshathabhyam,
namo nama sri guru padukhabyam. 9

ANANT SANSAAR SAMUDRA TAAR

dha 1	tin 2	tin 3	ta 4	dhin 5	dhin 6	dha 1	tin 2	tin 3	ta 4	dhin 5	dhin 6
P a	D nn	P -t	S' sn	S' sa	S' -r	D s	D mu	S' -dr	P ta	P r	-
R nau	P ka	D -yi	P ta	G bhyam	- -	GG guru	R bh	S -kti	R da	P bhyam	- -
D vai	D ra	P -gy	D sa	D mra	D -jy	S' d	D pu	P -j	D na	S' bhyam	-
G' n	G' mo	R' -n	G' m	G' h	G' sri	R'G' guru	R' pa	S' -du	R' ka	G' bhyam	-
R' n	R' mo	S' -n	R' m	R' h	S' sri	G'R' guru	S' pa	-D -du	S' ka	S' bhyam	-
S k	R vi	S -tv	R va	P ra	P -shi	P ni	D sha	S' -k	D ra	P bhyam	-
M daur	P bha	D -gy	P da	M van	- -	RM bud	R ma	S -li	R ka	M bhyam	-
MP du	DS' ri	D -kri	S' ta	S' n	R' -mr	R' vi	R' p	M' -tti	S' ta	S' bhyam	-
P n	P mo	M -n	D m	D h	D sri	PP guru	M pa	R -du	M ka	M bhyam	-
M n	R' mo	S' -n	R' m	R' h	R' sri	M'M' guru	S' pa	D -du	S' ka	S' bhyam	-
P n	P mo	M -n	D m	D h	D sri	PP guru	M pa	R -du	M ka	M bhyam	-
											M -n

M	P	M	D	D	S'	NS'	ND	D	N	S'S'	M
ta	-	y	yo	h	sri	pti	tam	-s	mi	yuh	-k
G	M	G	RG	P	P	D	-	P	G	P	M
da	chi	-d	pya	shu	-d	ri	-	-dr	vr	ya	-h
S'	N	P	N	N	N	S'S'	N	D	S'	S'	-
mu	ka	-shch	va	ch	-s	pti	tam	-hi	ta	bhyam	-
S'	R'	S'	R'	R'	R'	G'G'	R'	S'	R'	G'	-
n	mo	-n	m	h	sri	guru	pa	-du	ka	bhyam	-
R'	G'	R'	G'	G'	R'	G'G'	R'	S'	R'	G'	-
n	mo	-n	m	h	sri	guru	pa	-du	ka	bhyam	-

music: G'- R'- S'- P- D- MPDS'
         G'- R' –R'S' DS'P-

P	D	P	S'	S'	S'	D	D	S'	P	P	-
na	li	-k	ni	ka	-sh	p	da	-hr	ta	bhyam	-
R	P	D	P	G	G	G	R	S	R	P	-
na	na	-vi	mo	ha	-di	ni	va	-ri	ka	bhyam	-
D	D	P	D	D	D	S'	D	P	D	S'	-
n	m	-jj	na	bhi	-sht	t	ti	-pr	da	bhyam	-
G'	G'	R'	G'	G'	G'	R'G'	R'	S'	R'	G'	-
n	mo	-n	m	h	sri	guru	pa	-du	ka	bhyam	-
R'	R'	S'	R'	R'	S'	G'R'	S'	-D	S'	S'	-
n	mo	-n	m	h	sri	guru	pa	-du	ka	bhyam	-
S	RM	RS	R	P	-	DD	D	S'	D	P	-
nri	pa	-li	mau	hi	-	brij	r	-tn	kan	ti	-
M	P	D	P	M	-	RM	R	S	R	M	-
s	ri	-dwi	ra	jn	-	jhsh	k	-ny	ka	bhyam	-
MP	D	S'	D	S'	S'	R'R'	R'	M'	S'	S'	-
nri	p	-tv	da	bhyam	-	nt	lo	-k	pn	kte	-

P	P	M	D	D	D	PP	M	R	M	M	-
n	mo	-n	m	h	sri	guru	pa	-du	ka	bhyam	-
M	R'	S'	R'	R'	R'	M'M'	S'	D	S'	S'	-
n	mo	-n	m	h	sri	guru	pa	-du	ka	bhyam	-
P	P	-M	D	D	D	PP	M	-R	M	M	-
n	mo	-n	m	h	sri	guru	pa	-du	ka	bhyam	-
M	MP	-P	P	PD	D	S'	N	-D	N	S'	-
pa	paan	-dh	ka	ra	-rk	p	rn	-p	ra	bhyam	-
M	G	-R	G	P	P	P	D	-P	G	PM	-
ta	p	-tr	ya	hin	-dr	kh	ge	-shv	ra	bhyam	-
S'	N	P	N	N	N	S'	N	-D	S'	S'	-
ja	iya	bdhi	sn	sho	-sh	n	va	-d	va	bhyam	-
S'	R'	-S'	R'	R'	R'	G'G'	R'	-S'	R'	G'	-
n	mo	-n	m	h	sri	guru	pa	-du	ka	bhyam	-
R'	G'	-R'	G'	G'	R'	G'G'	R'	-S'	R'	G'	-
n	mo	-n	m	h	sri	guru	pa	-du	ka	bhyam	-
P	D	-P	S'	S'S'	S'	D	-	-S'	P	P	-
sh	ma	-di	sht	kpr	d	vai	-	-bh	va	bhyam	-
R	P	-D	P	G	-	GG	R	S	R	P	-
s	ma	-dhi	da	n	-	brt	di	kshi	ta	bhyam	-
D	D	-P	D	D	D	DS'	D	-P	D	S'	-
mu	kte	-he	he	tu	shch	sthir	bh	kti	da	bhyam	-
G'	G'	-R'	G'	G'	G'	R'G'	R'	-S'	R'	G'	-
n	mo	-n	m	h	sri	guru	pa	-du	ka	bhyam	-
R'	R'	-S'	R'	R'	S'	G'R'	S'	-D	S'	S'	-
n	mo	-n	m	h	sri	guru	pa	-du	ka	bhyam	-
S	R	-S	R	P	-	DD	D	S'	P	P	-
swa	rcha	-p	ra	na	-	mkhi	le	sht	da	bhyam	-

Vinod Kumar

M	P	-D	P	M	M	R	M	-R	S	RM	-
swa	ha	-s	ha	y	-ksh	dhu	rn	-dh	ra	bhyam	-
MP	D	-P	S'	S'	S'S'	R'	-	M'	S'	S'	-
swan	ta	-ksh	bha	v	prd	pu	-	-j	na	bhyam	-
P	P	-M	D	D	D	PP	M	-R	M	M	-
n	mo	-n	m	h	sri	guru	pa	-du	ka	bhyam	-
M	R'	-S'	R'	R'	R'	M'M'	S'	-D	S'	S'	-
n	mo	-n	m	h	sri	guru	pa	-du	ka	bhyam	-
P	P	-M	D	D	D	PP	M	-R	M	M	-
n	mo	-n	m	h	sri	guru	pa	-du	ka	bhyam	-
G	MP	MP	D	D	DD	N	-	D	S'	S'	-
ka	ma	-di	s	rp	brj	ga	-	ru	na	bhyam	-
M	G	-R	G	P	P	M	D	-P	G	PM	-
vi	ve	-k	vai	ra	gy	ni	dhi	-pr	da	bhyam	-
S'	N	-P	N	N	-	R'S'	N	-D	S'	S'	-
bo	dh	-pr	da	bhyam	-	drut	mo	-ksh	da	bhyam	-
S'	R'	-S'	R'	R'	R'	G'G'	R'	-S'	R'	G'	-
n	mo	-n	m	h	sri	guru	pa	-du	ka	bhyam	-
R'	G'	-R'	G'	G'	R'	G'G'	R'	-S'	R'	G'	-
n	mo	-n	m	h	sri	guru	pa	-du	ka	bhyam	-

3. AAO RANG LEN JEEVAN APNA

Radha Bhajan   Singer: Krishna das
Taal: Kaharwa Dugun   Chord: SGP   S=D#
https://youtu.be/tEcaHdSzQcg

aao rang lein jivan apna radha naam ki masti me
radha naam jape har rasna, ghar ghar basti basti me
radha radha radha radha radha radha
radha radha radha radha radha radha

aese rang me rang jayein jo fika kabhi padena
rang birnge jag ka jis par koii rang chadhe na
khud ki mita ke hasti mil jayein ham sab uski hasti me

Vinod Kumar

AAO RANG LEN JEEVAN APNA

dha	ge	n	ti	n	ke	dhi	n	dha	ge	n	ti	n	ke	dhi	n
1	2	3	4	5	6	7	8	1	2	3	4	5	6	7	8

```
GG    GG   P    GRS   RRS.N    SS    SG   G    GR   S
aao   rang len  jivn  apna-    radha nam  ki   masti me

GMD   DD   DM   DD    PPMPG
radha nam  jape har   rasna-,

GMD   DD   DM   DD    PPP-  PN   DP    MGR   MGR  S
radha nam  jape har   rasna-, ghar ghar  basti basti me

S'N   PD   ND   ND    MP    DP
radha radha radha radha radha radha

PPN   DP   MGR  GG    MGR   SS
radha- radha radha- radha ra-dha radha

PP   PP   MG  PP  PP  MG  DD  DND   PP   P—DM
aese rang me- rang jaen jo-  fika kabhi- pade na

PP   PPMG   PP  P  PP  MG DD  ND   PP   P –DM
rang birange- jag ka jis  par koii rang chadhe na

S'S'  S' S'S'  S'  NN  S'N DP  PN   DP  MGR MGR S
khud  ki mita  ke  hasti mil jaein ham sab  uski hasti me
```

4. AAJ GOKUL ME DHUM MACHI

Krishna Bhajan

Lyrics: Vinod Kumar

Taal: Daadra

https://youtu.be/I2K_Z1BCXbU

Music: Vinod Kumar

Singer: Vinod Kumar &Family

Chord: .NRM   S=C#

aaj gokul me dhum machi aaj har dil deevana hai
kanhaiya ko sajaana hai, janmotsav manaana hai
aaj gokul me dhum machi

१) tere mastane aake khade, aaj darshan to paana hai
    godi me utha ke tujhe, are jhula jhulana hai
    aaj gokul me dhum ….

२) bholi surat kanhaiya teri, mere man ko hai bhaye badi
    kajal ko lagaakar tujhe kala tika lagana hai
    aaj gokul me dhum ….

३) Mand muskan kanha teri, kashton ko mitaye meri
    tera gungaan gaate huye, jivan ko bitana hai
    aaj gokul me dhum ….

४) Janmon se tarasti thi main, is jag me bhatakti thi main
    charan mathe lagaana hai, bhav saagar tar jana hai
    aaj gokul me dhum ….

aaj gokul me, aaj mandir me
aaj ghar ghar me dhum machi aaj har dil divaana hai
knhaiya ko sajaana hai, janmotsav manaana hai
aaj gokul me dhum machi

hathi ghoda palki jay knhaiya laal ki

-'Vinod Kumar'

Vinod Kumar

AAJ GOKUL ME DHUM MACHI

dha 1	dhi 2	na 3	dha 4	tun 5	na 6	dha 1	dhi 2	na 3	dha 4	tun 5	na 6
									S aa	- -	S j
.N go	- -	R kul	- -	R me	- -	M dhu	- -	- -	G m	- -	G m
M chi	- -	- -	- -	- -	- -	- -	- -	- -	D aa	- -	D j
D h	- r	P di	N l	D di	- -	P va	- -	- -	G na	- -	- -
M hai	- -	- -	- -	- -	- -	G -	R -	- -	S kn	S hai	- -
.N ya	- -	R ko	- -	R s	- -	M ja	- -	- -	G na	- -	- -
M hai	- -	- -	- -	- -	- -	- -	- -	- -	D jan	- -	- -
P mo	- t	N s	- v	D m	- -	P na	- -	- -	G na	- -	- -
M hai	- -	- -	- -	- -	- -	G -	R -	- -	S aa	- -	S j
.N go	- -	R ku	- l	R me	- -	M dhu	- -	- -	G m	- -	G m
M chi	- -	- -	- -	- -	- -	- -	- -	- -			
									D te	D re	- -
D ms	- -	R' ta	- -	S' ne	- -	N aa	- -	D ke	- -	D kh	- -

N	-	-	-	-	-	D	P	-	M	-	M
de	-	-	-	-	-	-	-	-	aa	-	j
G	-	G	-	M	-	D	P	-	M	G	-
dr	-	shn	-	to	-	pa	-	-	na	-	-
M	-	-	-	-	-	G	R	-	S	-	-
hai	-	-	-	-	-	-	-	-	go	-	-
.N	-	R	-	R	-	M	-	G	-	G	-
di	-	me	-	u	-	tha	-	ke	-	tu	-
M	-	-	-	-	-	-	-	-	D	D	-
jhe	-	-	-	-	-	-	-	-	a	re	-
D	-	P	N	D	-	P	-	-	G	-	-
jhu	-	la	-	jhu	-	la	-	-	na	-	-
M	-	-	-	-	-	G	R	-			
hai	-	-	-	-	-	-	-	-			
									D	D	-
									bho	li	-
D	-	R'	-	S'	-	N	-	D	-	D	-
su	-	r	t	kn	-	hai	-	ya	-	te	-
N	-	-	-	-	-	D	P	-	M	M	-
ri	-	-	-	-	-	-	-	-	me	re	-
G	-	G	-	M	-	D	-	P	-	G	-
m	n	ko	-	hai	-	bha	-	ye	-	b	-
M	-	-	-	-	-	G	R	-	S	-	-
di	-	-	-	-	-	-	-	-	ka	-	-
.N	-	R	-	R	-	M	-	G	-	G	-
z	l	ko	-	l	-	ga	-	k	r	tu	-

Vinod Kumar

M	-	-	-	-	-	-	-	-	D	D	-
jhe	-	-	-	-	-	-	-	-	ka	la	-
D	-	P	N̲	D	-	P	-	-	G	-	-
ti	-	ka	-	l	-	ga	-	-	na	-	-
M	-	-	-	-	-	G̲	R	-			
hai	-	-	-	-	-	-	-	-			
									D	-	D
									mn	-	d
D	-	R'	-	S'	-	N̲	-	D	-	D	-
mu	s	ka	-	n	-	kan	-	ha	-	te	-
N̲	-	-	-	-	-	D	P	-	M	-	M
ri	-	-	-	-	-	-	-	-	k	-	sh
G	-	G	-	M	-	D	-	P	-	G	-
to	-	ko	-	mi	-	ta	-	ye	-	me	-
M	-	-	-	-	-	G̲	R	-	S	S	-
ri	-	-	-	-	-	-	-	-	te	ra	-
.N̲	-	R	-	R	-	M	-	G	-	G	-
gu	n	ga	-	n	-	ga	-	te	-	hu	-
M	-	-	-	-	-	-	-	-	D	-	-
e	-	-	-	-	-	-	-	-	ji	-	-
P	-	N̲	-	D	-	P	-	-	G	-	-
v	n	ko	-	bi	-	ta	-	-	na	-	-
M	-	-	-	-	-	G̲	R	-			
hai	-	-	-	-	-	-	-	-			
									D	-	-
									jn	-	-
D	-	R'	-	S'	-	N̲	-	D	-	D	-
mo	-	se	-	t	-	r	s	ti	-	thi	-
N̲	-	-	-	-	-	D	P	-	M	M	-
main	-	-	-	-	-	-	-	-	i	s	-

G	G	G	-	M	-	D	P	M	-	G	-
j	g	me	-	bh	-	t	k	ti	-	thi	-
M	-	-	-	-	-	G̲	R	-	S	S	-
main	-	-	-	-	-	-	-	-	ch	r	n
.N	-	R	-	R	-	M	-	-	G	-	-
ma	-	the	-	l	-	ga	-	-	na	-	-
M	-	-	-	-	-	-	-	-	D	D	-
hai	-	-	-	-	-	-	-	-	bh	v	-
P	-	N̲	-	D	-	P	-	-	G	-	-
sa	-	gr		tr	-	ja	-	-	na	-	-
M	-	-	-	-	-	G̲	R	-			
hai	-	-	-	-	-	-	-	-			
									S	-	S
									aa	-	j
.N	-	R	-	R	-	-	-	-	S	-	S
go	-	ku	l	me	-	-	-	-	aa	-	j
.N	-	R	-	R	-	-	-	-	S	-	S
mn	-	di	r	me	-	-	-	-	aa	-	j
.N	-	R	-	R	-	M	-	-	G	-	G
gh	r	gh	r	me	-	dhu	-	-	m	-	m
M	-	-	-	-	-	-	-	-	D	-	D
chi	-	-	-	-	-	-	-	-	aa	-	j
D	-	P	N̲	D	-	P	-	-	G	-	-
h	r	di	l	di	-	va	-	-	na	-	-
M	-	-	-	-	-	G̲	R	-	S	S	-
hai	-	-	-	-	-	-	-	-	kn	hai	-
.N	-	R	-	R	-	M	-	-	G	-	-
ya	-	ko	-	s	-	ja	-	-	na	-	-

Vinod Kumar

M	-	-	-	-	-	-	-	-	D	-	-
hai	-	-	-	-	-	-	-	-	jn	-	-
P	-	N	-	D	-	P	-	-	G	-	-
mo	t	s	v	m	-	na	-	-	na	-	-
M	-	-	-	-	-	G	R	-	S	-	S
hai	-	-	-	-	-	-	-	-	aa	-	j
.N	-	R	-	R	-	M	-	-	G	-	G
go	-	ku	I	me	-	dhu	-	-	m	-	m
M	-	-	-	-	-	-	-	-			
chi	-	-	-	-	-	-	-	-			
D	D	-	D	D	-	M	-	M	M	-	-
(ha	thi	-	gho	da	-	pa	-	I	ki	-	-
R	-	R	R	M	-	S	-	S	.N		
jy	-	kn	hai	ya	-	la	-	I	ki	-	-)x3

5. BANSI WALE KE CHARNO ME

Krishna Bhajan
Taal: Kaharwa
https://youtu.be/1Du-5K2WJ8g

Singer: Nikunj Kaamra
Chord: SM RP   S=C#

bansi vale ke charno me sar ho mera
fir na puchho ke us waqt kya baat hai
unke dware pe daala hai jab se dera
fir na puchho ke kaisi mulaqat hai

ye na chahun ke mujh ko khudayi mile
ye na chahun mujhe badshahi mile
khak dar ki mile ye muqaddar mera
isse badhkar bataao kya saugaat hai

ho gulami agar aali darbaar ki
yeh khudayi bhi hai badshaahi bhi hai
dasi dar ki bhikharin bane jis waqat

isse badhkar bataao ki kya baat hai

govind mero hai gopal mero hai|

sri banke bihari nndlal mero hai||

BANSI WALE KE CHARNO ME

dha	ge	n	ti	n	ke	dhi	n	dha	ge	n	ti	n	ke	dhi	n
1	2	3	4	5	6	7	8	1	2	3	4	5	6	7	8
												.P	-	.N	-
												bn	-	si	-
S	-	-	S	-	-	S	-	S	-	-	S/M	-	-	R	-
va	-	-	le	-	-	ke	-	chr	-	-	no	-	-	me	-
.N	-	-	R	-	-	R	-	R	-	-	-	P	-	P	-
sr	-	-	ho	-	-	me	-	ra	-	-	-	fi	r	na	-
P	-	-	M	-	-	R	-	S	.N	-	R	-	-	R	-
pu	-	-	chho	-	-	ke	-	u	s	-	v	-	k	t	-
S	-	-	S	-	-	S	-	S	-	-	-	.P	-	.N	-
kya	-	-	ba	-	-	t	-	hai	-	-	-	u	n	ke	-
S	-	-	S	-	-	S	-	S	-	-	S/M	-	-	R	-
dwa	-	-	re	-	-	pe	-	da	-	-	la	-	-	hai	-
.N	-	-	R	-	-	R	-	R	-	-	-	P	-	P	-
j	b	-	se	-	-	de	-	ra	-	-	-	fi	r	na	-
P	-	-	M	-	-	R	-	.N	-	-	R	-	-	R	-
pu	-	-	chho	-	-	ki	-	kai	-	-	si	-	-	mu	-
S	-	-	S	-	-	S	-	S	-	-	-				
la	-	-	ka	-	-	t	-	hai	-	-	-				
												R	-	M	-
												ye	-	na	-

Vinod Kumar

P	-	-	P	-	-	P	-	M	P	-	R	-	-	M	-
cha	-	-	hun	-	-	ke	-	mu	jh	-	ko	-	-	khu	-
P	-	-	P	-	-	P	-	P	-	-	-	P	-	P	-
da	-	-	ii	-	-	mi	-	le	-	-	-	ye	-	na	-
P	-	-	M	-	-	R	-	.N	-	-	R	-	-	R	-
cha	-	-	hun	-	-	mu	-	jhe	-	-	ba	-	-	d	-
S	-	-	S	-	-	S	-	S	-	-	-	.P	-	.N	-
sha	-	-	hi	-	-	mi	-	le	-	-	-	kha	-	k	-
S	-	-	S	-	-	S	-	S	-	-	-	S/M	-	R	-
dr	-	-	ki	-	-	mi	-	le	-	-	-	ye	-	mu	-
.N	-	-	R	-	-	R	-	R	-	-	-	P	-	P	-
q	-	-	dd	r	-	me	-	ra	-	-	-	i	s	se	-
P	-	-	M	-	-	R	-	.N	-	-	R	-	-	R	-
b	dh	-	k	-	r	b	-	ta	-	-	o	-	-	kya	-
S	-	-	S	-	-	S	-	S	-	-	-	R	-	M	-
sau	-	-	ga	-	-	t	-	hai	-	-	-	ho	-	gu	-
P	-	-	P	-	-	P	-	M	P	-	R	-	-	M	-
la	-	-	mi	-	-	a	-	g	r	-	aa	-	-	li	-
P	-	-	P	-	-	P	-	P	-	-	-	P	-	P	-
d	r	-	ba	-	-	r	-	ki	-	-	-	ye	-	khu	-
P	-	-	M	-	-	R	-	.N	-	-	-	R	-	R	-
da	-	-	yi	-	-	bhi	-	hai	-	-	-	ba	-	d	-
S	-	-	S	-	-	S	-	S	-	-	-	.P	-	.N	-
sha	-	-	hi	-	-	bhi	-	hai	-	-	-	da	-	si	-
S	-	-	S	-	-	S	-	S	-	-	S/M	-	-	R	-
dr	-	-	ki	-	-	bhi	-	kha	-	-	rn	-	-	b	-
.N	-	-	R	-	-	R	-	R	-	R	-	P	-	P	-
ne	-	-	ji	-	-	s	-	v	-	qt	-	i	s	se	-

P	-	-	M	-	-	R	-	.N	-	-	R	-	-	R	-
b	dh	-	k	-	r	b	-	ta	-	-	o	-	-	ki	-
S	-	-	S	-	-	S	-	S	-	-	-				
kya	-	-	ba	-	-	t	-	hai	-	-	-				
														S	-
														go	-
.N	-	-	.N	S	-	R	-	R	-	M	-	G	-	G	-
vin	-	-	d	me	-	ro	-	hai	-	-	-	-	-	go	-
M	-	-	R	R	-	S	-	S	-	-	-	-	-	P	-
pa	-	-	l	me	-	ro	-	hai	-	-	-	-	-	sri	-
P	-	D	P	-	-	M	-	G	-	G	-	R	-	R	-
ban	-	-	ke	-	-	bi	-	ha	-	ri	-	nn	-	d	-
G	-	-	G	R	-	S	-	S	-	-	-	-	-	S	-
la	-	-	l	me	-	ro	-	hai	-	-	-	-	-	go	-
.N	-	-	-	R	-	S	-	S	-	-	-	-	-	S	-
vin	-	-	d	me	-	ro	-	hai	-	-	-	-	-	go	-
.N	-	-	-	R	-	S	-	S	-	-	-	-	-	M	-
pa	-	-	l	me	-	ro	-	hai	-	-	-	-	-	go	-
G	-	-	M	R	-	S	-	S	-	-	-	-	-	M	-
vin	-	-	d	me	-	ro	-	hai	-	-	-	-	-	go	-
M	-	-	-	R	-	S	-	S	-	-	-	-	-		
pa	-	-	l	me	-	ro	-	hai	-	-	-	-	-		

Vinod Kumar

6. BRIJ ME RATAN RADHIKA GORI

Radha Bhajan
Lyrics: Madhup
Taal: Kaharwa Dugun
https://youtu.be/2onj3z4TenE

Music: Tinu Singh
Singer: Tinu Singh
Chord: GPN PNR'   S=C#

sab rasikan ki pranan pyari,
brij mandal sarkar hai radha
raseshvari ras rup ujiyari,
brij lila aadhaar hai radha
madhup hari gulam hai jisko
asht sakhiyan sardaar hai radha

brij me ratan radhika gori
radhika gori, radhika gori,
o brij me ratan radhika gori

kumud kali rasmayi rasbhori
ati krunamayi kamal kishori
priye vadini madhur bhashini
swarn lata ati gori
brij me -3 ratan radhika gori,

ras swamini radha rani
sant bhakt rasikan maharani
ati badbhagin sadaa suhagin
barsane ki chhori, brij me -3 ratan radhika gori,

sab sukh saar parmdhan radha
radha naam hare har baadha
kahen 'mdhup' kar paan radha ras
baje bans ki pori, brij me -3 ratan radhika gori,
radha radha radha radha radha radha ra-dha-
radha radha ra-dha-

BRIJ ME RATAN RADHIKA GORI

dha -ti na ghena	dha -ti na ghena	dha -ti na ghena	dha -ti na ghena
1 2 3 4	5 6 7 8	1 2 3 4	5 6 7 8

R'R'   R'R'R'R'   S'N S'G'R'R'   R' R'
sab   rasikan   ki- pra-nn   pyari

G'G' G'G'G'   G'G' G'P'G'P' G'   R'R'
brij   mandal   sar ka--r   hai radha

G'G'G'G'   R'S'   G'   R'S'ND
raseshvari ras   rup ujiyari

DD   DS'   S'N   D   PP
brij lila aadhar hai radha

G'G'G'   G'G'   S'S'G'R' S' NDN-D
madhup   hari gula-m   hai jisko—

S'S'   S'S'S'   S' DN   D   PP
asht   skhiyan sardar hai radha

											P
												o
G	P	P	D	D	N	N	D	-	D P G	P	- P	-
bri	j	me	-	r	t	n	ra	-	dhi ka	-	go - ri	-
-	S'	S'	S'	R'	G'	-	-	-	- - -	R'	M' G'	R'
-	ra	dhi	ka	go	ri	-	-	-	- - -	ii	ii ii	ii
S'	N	D	P	D	P	-	P	G	P P	R'	R' -	P
ii	ii	ii	ii	ii	ii	-	o	bri	j me	jy	ho -	o
G	P	P	-	R'	R'	-	P	G	P P D	D	N N	D
bri	j	me	-	jy	ho	-	o	bri	j me	r	t n	ra
-	D	P	G	P	-	P	-	-	- - -	G'	G' R'	G'
-	dhi	ka	-	go	-	ri	-2	-	- - -	go	ri ii	ii

Vinod Kumar

R'	-	R'	-
ii	-	ii	-

interlude: R G P- P- P-   R G D – D- D-
               P D N- D- N- D-   P- P- P- x2

S'	S'	S'	S'	G'	-	G'	G'	R'	M'	G'	R'	R'	-	R'	-
ku	mu	d	k	li	-	r	s	m	yi	r	s	bho	-	ri	-

S'	S'	S'	S'	G'	-	G'	G'	R'	M'	G'	R'	R'	-	R'	-
a	ti	k	ru	na	-	m	yi	k	m	l	ki	sho	-	ri	-

G'	G'	-	G'	-	G'	G'	-	R'	R'	R'	G'	R'	S'	S'	-
pri	ye	-	va	-	di	ni	-	m	dhu	r	bha	-	shi	ni	-

R'	M'	M'	G'	G'	-	R'	R'	S'	-	S'	-	N	-	D	P
sw	r	n	l	ta	-	a	ti	go	-	ri	-	-	-	-	-

-	-	-	-	G	P	P	-	R'	R'	-	P	G	P	P	-
-	-	-	-	bri	j	me	-	jy	ho	-	o	bri	j	me	-

R'	R'	-	P	G	P	P	-	D	N	N	D	-	D	P	G
jy	ho	-	o	bri	j	me	-	r	t	n	ra	-	dhi	ka	-

P	-	P	-
go	-	ri	-

interlude: R G P- P- P-   R G D – D- D-
               P D N- D- N- D-   P- P- P- x2

S'	-	S'	G'	-	G'	G'	R'	M'	-	G'	R	R'	-	R'	-
ra	-	s	swa	-	mi	ni	-	ra	-	dha	-	ra	-	ni	-

S'	-	S'	G'	-	G'	G'	R'	M'	M'	G'	R'	R'	-	R'	-
sn	-	t	bh	-	kt	r	si	k	n	m	ha	ra	-	ni	-

P'	-	P'	P'	-	M'	G'	G'	M'	M'	G'	G'	R'	-	R'	-
sn	-	t	bh	-	kt	r	si	k	n	m	ha	ra	-	ni	-

G'	G'	G'	G'	G'	-	G'	G'	R'	R'	-	G'	R'	-	S'	S'
a	ti	b	d	bha	-	g	n	s	da	-	su	ha	-	g	n

R'	M'	M'	-	G'	-	R'	-	S'	-	S'	-	N	-	D	P
b	r	sa	-	ne	-	ki	-	chho	-	ri	-	-	-	-	-

-	-	-	-	G	P	P	-	R'	R'	-	P	G	P	P	-
-	-	-	-	bri	j	me	-	jy	ho	-	o	bri	j	me	-
R'	R'	-	P	G	P	P	-	D	N	N	D	-	D	P	G
jy	ho	-	o	bri	j	me	-	r	t	n	ra	-	dhi	ka	-
P	-	P	-												
go	-	ri	-												

interlude: R G P- P- P-   R G D – D- D-
P D N- D- N- D-   P- P- P- x2

S'	S'	S'	S'	G'	-	G'	G'	R'	M'	G'	R'	R'	-	R'	-
s	b	su	kh	sa	-	r	p	r	m	dh	n	ra	-	dha	-
S'	-	S'	-	G'	-	G'	R'	M'		G'	R'	R'	-	R'	-
ra	-	dha	-	na	-	m	h	re	-	h	r	ba	-	dha	-
G'	G'	-	G'	G'	G'	G'	G'	R'	-	R'	G'	R'	-	S'	S'
ka	hen	-	m	dhu	p	k	r	pa	-	n	ra	dha	-	r	s
R'	M'	-	G'	-	R'	R'	-	S'	-	S'	-	N	-	D	P
b	je	-	ban	-	s	ki	-	po	-	ri	-	-	-	-	-
-	-	-	-	G	P	P	-	R'	R'	-	P	G	P	P	-
-	-	-	-	bri	j	me	-	jy	ho	-	o	bri	j	me	-
R'	R'	-	P	G	P	P	-	D	N	N	D	-	D	P	G
jy	ho	-	o	bri	j	me	-	r	t	n	ra	-	dhi	ka	-
P	-	P	-	-	-	-	P	P	P	P	P	P	P	P	P
go	-	ri	-	-	-	-	sri	ra	dha	ra	dha	ra	dha	ra	dha
N	N	D	D	P	-	P	-	(PNR') Chord play							
ra	dha	ra	dha	ra	-	dha	-x4	ra dha ra dha				ra	-	dha	-x4

Vinod Kumar

7. CHHAVI DEKH TUMHARI MANMOHAN

Krishna Bhajan (2021)   Music: Vinod Kumar
Lyrics: Vinod Kumar   Singer: Abhishek Bhama, Muskan,
Taal: Kaharwa   Vinod
   Chord: GM*N   S=C#
krishna bhajan: https://youtu.be/gDe6F6GYGLE

chhavi dekh tumhari man mohan, dil prem neer me bhig gaya

aaye hain dar pe bhakt tumhaare, aas ki jyot jalaaye hue
aaj prabhu teri kirpa barse, vanshi se meethe geet suna

CHHAVI DEKH TUMHARI MANMOHAN

dha	-	ta	ta	ta	-	dha	dha	dha	-	ta	ta	ta	-	dha	dha
1	2	3	4	5	6	7	8	1	2	3	4	5	6	7	8
														M*	M
														chh	vi
R	-	R	R	S	R	.N	S	G	G	G	-	G	G	S	G
de	-	kh	tun	ha	-	ri	-	m	n	mo	-	h	n	di	l
M	-	M	M	-	M	M*	N	M*	-	M	M	G	-		
pre	-	m	ni	-	r	me	-	bhi	-	g	g	ya	-		
	N	N	S'	S'	S'	S'	-	-	M*	M*	M*	M	M*	M	G
	aa	ye	hain	d	r	pe	-	-	bh	kt	tu	mha	-	re	-
-	N	N	N	D	N	D	M*	M	M*	M	G	M	M*	N	-
-	aa	s	ki	jyo	-	t	j	la	-	ye	hu	e	-	-	-
-	M*	M*	M*	M*	-	M*	M*	-	MM*	M	G	G	G	G	S
-	aa	j	pr	hu	-	te	ri	-	kir	pa	-	b	r	se	-
-	S	G	G	M	-	M*	N	M*	-	M	M	G	-		
-	vn	shi	se	mi	-	the	-	gi	-	t	su	na	-		

8. DAM DAM DAMRU BAAJE

Shiv Bhajan	Singer: Hari Om Sharan
Taal: Kaharwa	Chord: SGP S=E

https://youtu.be/c0UWiv_XNhc

dam dam dam dam damru baaje
jai shanker kailaash pati-2

bhav taarak hai naam tihaara, deen anathon ka rakhwala
puran parmanand prakaashi, akhileshvar bhagtan sukhraashi
jai shanker kailaash pati-2

jai jai kaar kare nar naari,bhola bhandaari bhola bhandaari
bhola bhandaari namah shivaay, daya karo bhola bhandaari
puran brahm sadaa avinaashi, yogeshvar mam hridaya nivaasi
jai shanker kailaash pati-2

DAM DAM DAMRU BAAJE

dha	ge	n	ti	n	ke	dhi	n	dha	ge	n	ti	n	ke	dhi	n
1	2	3	4	5	6	7	8	1	2	3	4	5	6	7	8
S	-	S	G	G	-	G	-	G	M	M	P	P	-	P	-
d	m	d	m	d	m	d	m	d	m	ru	-	ba	-	je	-
P	-	-	-	P	-	-	-	P	-	-	-	M	G	R	-
-	-	-	-	-	-	-	-	-	-	-	-	-	-	-	-
S	-	S	G	G	-	G	-	G	M	M	P	P	-	P	-
d	m	d	m	d	m	d	m	d	m	ru	-	ba	-	je	-
-	-	S	-	-	R	-	-	G	-	G	-	G	M	P	-
-	-	jai	-	-	shn	-	-	k	-	r	-	kai	-	-	-
-	-	G	-	-	R	-	S	S	-	-	-	R	-	.N	-
-	-	la	-	-	sh	-	p	ti	-	-	-	ii	-	ii	-

Vinod Kumar

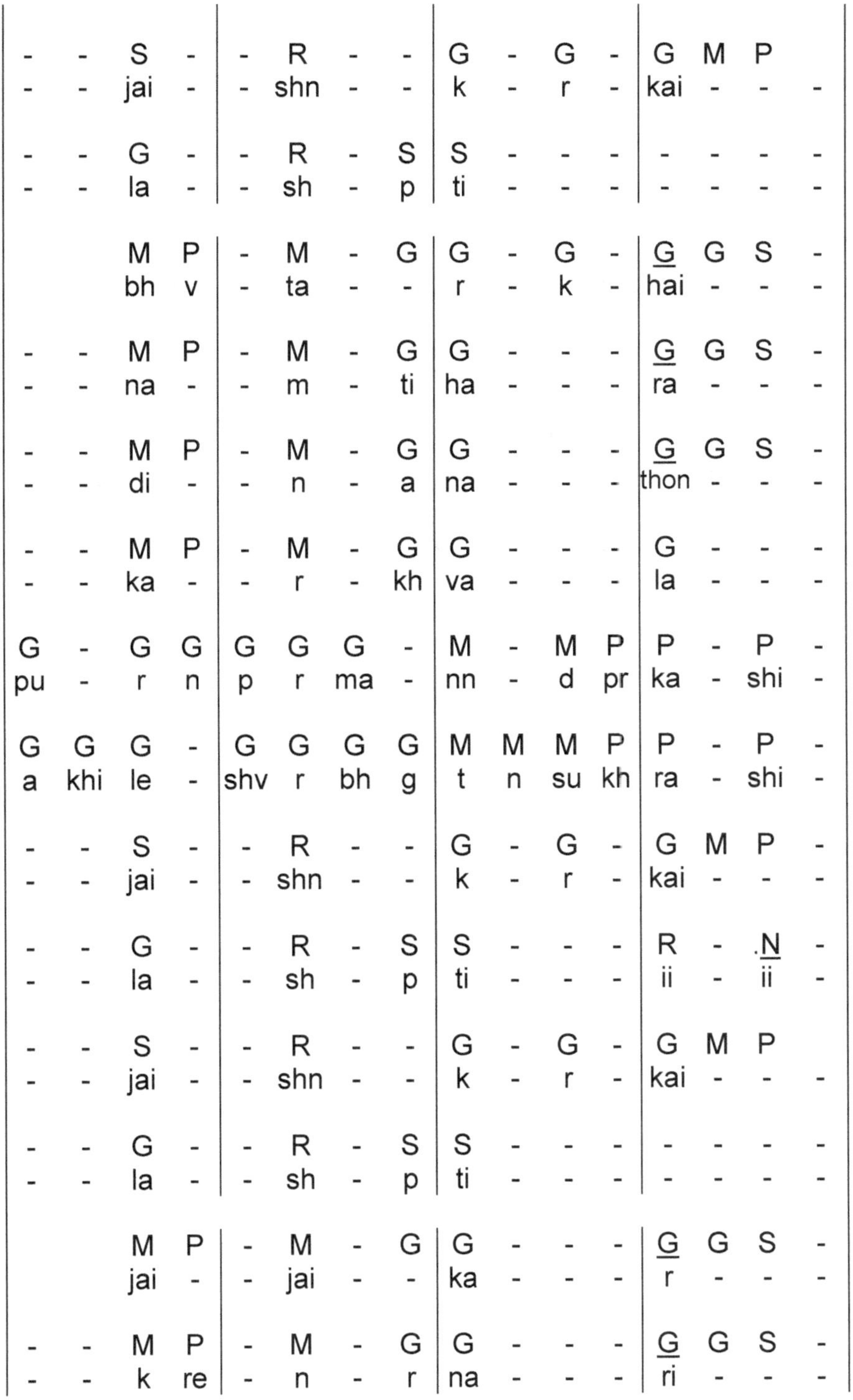

-	-	S	-	-	R	-	-	G	-	G	-	G	M	P	
-	-	jai	-	-	shn	-	-	k	-	r	-	kai	-	-	-
-	-	G	-	-	R	-	S	S	-	-	-	-	-	-	-
-	-	la	-	-	sh	-	p	ti	-	-	-	-	-	-	-
		M	P	-	M	-	G	G	-	G	-	G̲	G	S	-
		bh	v	-	ta	-	-	r	-	k	-	hai	-	-	-
-	-	M	P	-	M	-	G	G	-	-	-	G̲	G	S	-
-	-	na	-	-	m	-	ti	ha	-	-	-	ra	-	-	-
-	-	M	P	-	M	-	G	G	-	-	-	G̲	G	S	-
-	-	di	-	-	n	-	a	na	-	-	-	thon	-	-	-
-	-	M	P	-	M	-	G	G	-	-	-	G	-	-	-
-	-	ka	-	-	r	-	kh	va	-	-	-	la	-	-	-
G	-	G	G	G	G	G	-	M	-	M	P	P	-	P	-
pu	-	r	n	p	r	ma	-	nn	-	d	pr	ka	-	shi	-
G	G	G	-	G	G	G	G	M	M	M	P	P	-	P	-
a	khi	le	-	shv	r	bh	g	t	n	su	kh	ra	-	shi	-
-	-	S	-	-	R	-	-	G	-	G	-	G	M	P	-
-	-	jai	-	-	shn	-	-	k	-	r	-	kai	-	-	-
-	-	G	-	-	R	-	S	S	-	-	-	R	-	.N̲	
-	-	la	-	-	sh	-	p	ti	-	-	-	ii	-	ii	-
-	-	S	-	-	R	-	-	G	-	G	-	G	M	P	
-	-	jai	-	-	shn	-	-	k	-	r	-	kai	-	-	-
-	-	G	-	-	R	-	S	S	-	-	-	-	-	-	-
-	-	la	-	-	sh	-	p	ti	-	-	-	-	-	-	-
		M	P	-	M	-	G	G	-	-	-	G̲	G	S	-
		jai	-	-	jai	-	-	ka	-	-	-	r	-	-	-
-	-	M	P	-	M	-	G	G	-	-	-	G̲	G	S	-
-	-	k	re	-	n	-	r	na	-	-	-	ri	-	-	-

M	-	P	M	-	G	G	-	G	-	G	G	-	G	S	-
bho	-	la	bhn	-	da	ri	-	bho	-	la	bhn	-	da	ri	-
M	-	P	M	-	G	G	-	G	G	-	G	G	-	-	-
bho	-	la	bhn	-	da	ri	-	n	mah	-	shi	va	-	-	y
-	-	M	P	-	-	M	-	G	-	-	-	G̲	G	S	-
-	-	d	ya	-	-	k	-	ro	-	-	-	bho	-	-	-
-	-	M	P	-	M	-	G	G	-	-	-	G	-	-	-
-	-	la	-	-	bhn	-	-	da	-	-	-	ri	-	-	-
G	-	G	G	G	G	G	G	M	-	M	P	P	-	P	-
pu	-	r	n	br	h	m	s	da	-	a	vi	na	-	shi	-
G	-	G	-	G	G	G	G	M	M	M	P	P	-	P	-
yo	-	ge	-	shv	r	m	m	hri	d	y	ni	va	-	si	-
-	-	S	-	-	R	-	-	G	-	G	-	G	M	P	-
-	-	jai	-	-	shn	-	-	k	-	r	-	kai	-	-	-
-	-	G	-	-	R	-	S	S	-	-	-	R	-	.N	-
-	-	la	-	-	sh	-	p	ti	-	-	-	ii	-	ii	-
-	-	S	-	-	R	-	-	G	-	G	-	G	M	P	-
-	-	jai	-	-	shn	-	-	k	-	r	-	kai	-	-	-
-	-	G	-	-	R	-	S	S	-	-	-	-	-	-	-
-	-	la	-	-	sh	-	p	ti	-	-	-	-	-	-	-

Vinod Kumar

9. DEV MOGHRA KALI ME

Taal: Kaharwa   Chord: M$\underline{D}$S'   S= C#

https://youtu.be/vJR6Wj-TVLw

dev moghra kali me bhairo rang gayo re -2
dev moghra ki latpat daar,
dev moghra kali me bhairo rang gayo re

dev kahaa lagaun maruaa moghra re
dev kahaa laal anaar,
dev moghra kali me bhairo rang gayo re

dev bhuvan lgaun maruaa moghra re
dev angna me laal anaar,
dev moghra kali me bhairo rang gayo re

dev kahe se siinchun maruaa moghra re
dev kahe se laal anaar,
dev moghra kali me bhairo rang gayo re

dev dudhuan siinchun maruaa moghra re
dev imrat laal anaar,
dev moghra kali me bhairo rang gayo re

dev nau rang fule maruaa moghra re
dev das rang laal anaar,
dev moghra kali me bhairo rang gayo re

dev bhairo ko chdhaun maruaa moghra re
viir lngure ko laal anaar,
dev moghra kali me bhairo rang gayo re

DEV MOGHRA KALI ME

dha	ge	n	ti	n	ke	dhi	na	dha	ge	n	ti	n	ke	dhi	na
1	2	3	4	5	6	7	8	1	2	3	4	5	6	7	8

prelude:
MM DS' ---- M' G' R' S'-----
N S' G' R' S' N
D – P M M G D – P M

														D	D
														de	v
D	-D	D	D	D	D	P	M	P	M	M	M	M	-	D	D
mo	-gh	ra	k	li	me	bhai	ro	ra	m	g	yo	re	-	de	v
D	-D	D	D	D	D	N	N	N	-	D	-	P	-	D	D
mo	-gh	ra	ki	l	t	p	t	da	-	-	-	r	-	de	v
D	-D	D	D	D	D	P	M	P	M	M	M	M	-		
mo	-gh	ra	k	li	me	bhai	ro	r	m	g	yo	re	-		

interlude:
S' --- NS' NS' R'S'ND
N --- DN DN S'NDP
D --- PD PD NDPM M M ---

														M	M
														de	v
G	G	-	G	M	D	gh	P	M	-	G	M	M	-	D	-
k	ha	-	l	ga	un	mru	aa	mo	-	gh	ra	re	-	ae	-
D	-	D	-	D	-	N	N	N	-	D	-	P	-	D	-
k	-	ha	-	la	-	l	a	na	-	aa	-	r	-	de	v
D	-D	D	D	D	D	P	M	P	M	M	M	M	-		
mo	-gh	ra	k	li	me	bhai	ro	r	m	g	yo	re	-		

interlude: S' --- NS' NS' R'S'ND
           N --- DN DN S'NDP

Vinod Kumar

D --- PD PD NDPM M M ---

M M
de v

G	G	G	G	M	D	D	P	M	-	G	M	M	-	D	-
bhu	v	n	l	ga	un	mru	aa	mo	-	gh	ra	re	-	ae	-

D	D	D	D	D	-	N	N	N	-	D	-	P	-	D	-
an	g	na	me	la	-	l	a	na	-	aa	-	r	-	de	v

D	-D	D	D	D	D	P	M	P	M	M	M	M	-
mo	-gh	ra	k	li	me	bhai	ro	r	m	g	yo	re	-

play rest as above—

MM GG G MD   DP   M GM M
dev kahe se siinchun maruaa mo ghra re

D DD D DN NN D P
ae kahe se lal ana - re,

D DDD DD D PM   PM   MM M
dev moghra kli me bhairo rang gyo re

MM MGGG   MD   DP   M GM M
dev dudhuan siinchun maruaa mo ghra re

D   DDDD DN NN D P
ae imart lal ana - r,   dev moghra kali .....

MM aMG GG   MD DP   M GM M
dev nau- rang fule mruaa mo ghra re

MD DD DD DNN NN D P
ae ds rng la-l ana - r, dev moghra kali ....

M GG G GMD   DP   M GM M
dev bhairo ko chdhaun mruaa mo ghra re

<u>D</u>   <u>DD</u>   <u>D</u> <u>DNN</u>   <u>NN</u> <u>D</u> P
viir langure ko la-l   ana - r, dev moghra kali

10.   DEVI STUTI

Taal: Kaharwa

Raag: Bhimpalasi
Chord: S<u>G</u>P   S=C#

jay devii durga gauri shankari parvati

bhuvana mohini lalita lakshmi kalaavati

jay devii durga gauri shankari parvati

kamal kamini hari narayani bhagvati

ved mata vidya dayini bharati

hans vahini viina pani saraswati

DEVI STUTI

dha	ge	n	ti	n	ke	dhi	n	dha	ge	n	ti	n	ke	dhi	n
1	2	3	4	5	6	7	8	1	2	3	4	5	6	7	8

SR   .<u>N</u>.N   RR   <u>GG</u>   RS.<u>N</u>   SSS
jay   devii   durga   gauri   shankari   parvati

SMM   MM<u>G</u>   MPM   <u>GG</u>   <u>G</u>R-.<u>N</u>SR<u>G</u>-
bhuvan   mohini   llita   lakshami   kalavati

<u>GG</u>   .<u>N</u>.N   RR   <u>GG</u>   RS.<u>N</u>   SSS
jay   devii   durga   gauri   shankari   parvati

PPM   PPP   MP   PM-RM   MP MP
kamal   kamini   hari   narayani   bhagvati

<u>NN</u>   <u>NN</u>   DD   P-MM   PDDP
ved   mata   vidya   dayini   bharti

PM   PDDD   MM   <u>GG</u>   MRSS
hans   vahini   viina   pani   saraswati

Vinod Kumar

11. DEVI STUTI 2

Taal: Bhajani Theka

Raag= Bhimpalasi
Chord: S$\underline{G}$P   S=.G

https://youtu.be/Ph3zjdE3XMg

devii.......... jag janani shakti mata

pranav   swarupini   praneshvari
devii.......... jag janani shakti mata

gyan   pradaayini   gyaneshvari
tripur   sundari   dakshayini
devii.......... jag janani shakti mata

bhagvati   bharti   narayani
devii   narayani devii narayani
devii.......... jag janani shakti mata

jagdishvari   jagnmohini
karunamayi   satya   narayani
devii.......... jag janani shakti mata

DEVI STUTI 2

dha	ge	na	ti	n	ke	dhin	n	dha	ge	na	ti	n	ke	dhin	n
1	2	3	4	5	6	7	8	1	2	3	4	5	6	7	8

S.NSGMP   GM PMG   R.N   SS
devii.........   jag janani   shakti mata

GG.N   SG-GG-   GMPPMGM-G-
pranav   swarupini   praneshvari

S.NSGMP   GM PMG   R.N   SS
devii.........   jag janani   shakti mata

MPN   PNNN   PNS'NPMPM-G-
gyan   pradayini   gyaneshvari

GMP   NS'S'S'   NS'S'S' NDN-P-M-
tripur   sundari   dakshayini

NS'G'G'   S'G'G'G'   NNS'S'S'
bhagvati   bharti   narayani

G'G'   NS'G'G'   NS'   NPNS'S'
devii   narayani   devii   narayani

S'S'NS'NP   PNS'NPMPM-G-
jagdishvari   jagnmohini

MPS'S'N   PP   MG.NS
karunamayi   satya   narayani

Vinod Kumar

12. GAAIYE GANPATI JAG VANDAN

Ganpati Bhajan
Taal: Kaharwa
https://youtu.be/Z-IkXNa-BpY

Singer: Md. Husain, Ahmed Husain
Chord: .NRP SGP GPN   S=C#

gaaiye ganpati jag vandan, shankar suvan bhawani nandan
shankar suvan....
gaaiye ganpati jag vandan

modak priya mud mangal data, vidya varidhi buddhi vidhata
shankar suvan....
gaaiye ganpati jag vandan

siddhi sadan gaj badan vinaayak, kripa sindhu sunder sab laayak
shankar suvan....
gaaiye ganpati jag vandan

maangat tulsidas kar jore, basahun raam siya maanas more
shankar suvan....
gaaiye ganpati jag vandan

GAAIYE GANPATI JAG VANDAN

dha	ge	na	ti	n	ke	dhin	n	dha	ge	na	ti	n	ke	dhin	n
1	2	3	4	5	6	7	8	1	2	3	4	5	6	7	8
	.N	-	R	G	R	G	P	G	R	G	M*	R	-	S	S
	ga	-	i	ye	-	g	n	p	ti	j	g	vn	-	d	n
-	P	P	P	P	P	P	P	M*	D	P	M*	R	S	R	.N
-	shn	k	r	su	v	n	bh	va	-	ni	-	nn	-	d	n
-	P	N	N	S'	S'	S'	S'	N	D	N	S'	N	D	N	P
-	mo	d	k	pri	y	mu	d	mn	-	g	l	da	-	ta	-
-	P	S'	-	N	-	D	P	-	P	P	G	R	-	G	-
-	vi	dya	-	va	-	ri	dhi	-	bu	ddhi	vi	dha	-	ta	-
-	P	N	N	S'	S'	S'	S'	N	D	N	S'	N	D	N	P
-	si	ddhi	s	d	n	g	j	b	d	n	vi	na	-	y	k
-	P	S'	N	-	D	P	-	P	P	G	R	G	-	G	G
-	kri	pa	sin	-	dhu	sun	-	d	r	s	b	la	-	y	k
-	P	-N	N	S'	S'	S'	S'	N	D	N	S'	N	D	N	P
-	maan	-g	t	tu	l	si	da	-	s	k	r	jo	-	re	-
-	PP	S'	N	-	D	P	P	P	-	P	P	G	R	G	-
-	bs	hun	ra	-	m	si	y	ma	-	n	s	mo	-	re	-

Vinod Kumar

13. GURU MAHIMA

Taal: Kaharwa

Raag: Based on Raag Dhani
Chord: SGP   S=D

https://youtu.be/e47J6NGwl7k   S G G̲ M P N̲ S'

gururbrahma   gururvishnu   gururdevo   maheshvrah
gururdev   parmbrahm   tasmai sri-- gurve namah

agyan timirandhasya gyananjan shalakya
chakshuru militam ye na tasmai shri gurve namah

akhand mandalakaram vyaptam ye na characharan
tatpadam darshitam ye na tamai shri gurve namah

anek janm samprapt karm bandha vidahine
aatmgyan pradanen tasmai shri gurve namah

mannathaah shri jagannatho madguru shri jagadguruh
mamatma sarv hutatma tamai shri gurve namah

brahmanandam param sukhadam kevalam gyan murtim
dvamdatitam gagan sadrasham tatv masya dilakshyam

ekam nityam vimalmachalam srvadhisakshihutam
bhavatitam trigunrahitam sadgurum tam namami

sadgurum tam namami sadgurum tam namami
sadgurum tam namami sadgurum tam namami

GURU MAHIMA

dha	ge	na	ti	n	ke	dhin	n	dha	ge	na	ti	n	ke	dhin	n
1	2	3	4	5	6	7	8	1	2	3	4	5	6	7	8

NS'S'S'   NNS'S'S'   NS'NNP   S'S'S'S'
gururbrahma   gururvishnu   gururdevo   maheshvrah

NS'NG'S'   NS'NPMG   GG MPN   NNP MMM
gururdev   parmbrahm   tasmai sri-- gurve namah

MPM   GGM MM   GSGGG   MPMP
agyan timirandhasya gyananjan shalakya

MPNPNNNS'   N PMG GG   MPN NNP MMM
chakshuru militam ye na-- tasmai shri gurve namah

NS'S'   S'S'S'S'S'   NS'   N P S'S'S'S'
akhand mandalakaram vyaptam ye na characharan

NS'S'   NS'N   P PMG GG   MPN NNP   MMM
tatpadam darshitam ye na--- tamai shri   gurve namah

MPMG GG   MMM   GS   GG   MPMP
anek   janm samprapt karm bandha vidahine

MPNN   NS'PPMG GG MPN NNP MMM
aatmgyan pradanen tasmai shri gurve namah

S'S'S'   S' NS'S'S'   NS'N   P PS'S'S'S'
mannathaah shri jagannatho madguru shri jagadguruh

NS'S'   NS' NPPMG GG MPN NNP MMM
mamatma sarv hutatma tamai shri gurve namah

MPGG   MMM MMM   SGGG GMPM PP
brahmanandam param sukhadam kevalam gyan   murtim

MPNNN   S'S'N   PPP   S'S' PP   GMM
dvamdatitam gagan sadrasham tatv masya dilakshyam

Vinod Kumar

MP<u>N</u>   <u>NN</u>   S'<u>N</u>PS'S'S'   S'S'S'<u>G</u>'<u>N</u>S'S' - <u>N</u>PM
ekam nityam vimalmachalam srvadhisakshihutam

S'<u>N</u>S'<u>G</u>'S'S' <u>G</u>'S'<u>N</u>S'S'P   S'-<u>N</u>P   M<u>G</u> PMM
bhavatitam trigunrahitam   sadgurum tam namami

S'<u>N</u>P   M<u>G</u> PMM   S<u>GGG</u>   MP<u>N</u> PMM
sadgurum tam namami sadgurum tam   namami

S'<u>N</u>P   M<u>G</u> PMM   S<u>GGG</u>   MP<u>N</u> PMM
sadgurum tam namami sadgurum tam   namami

14. GOPAL GOKUL VALLABHI

Bhajan   Music: Jagjit Singh
Tulsi Das   Singer: Jagjit Singh
Taal: Rupak   Chord: SGP   S=C
https://youtu.be/xPuqyNwpJ5I

gopal gokul vallabhi priya gop gosut vallabham
charnaarvind maham bhaje, bhajniya sur muni durlabham

ghanshyam kaa anek chhavi lokabhira manoharam
kinjalik vasan kishor murti muul gun karunakaram

sirkeki pachchh vilol kundal arun vanruh lochanam
gunlavtams vichitr sab ang dhatu bhav bhaya mochanam

kach kutil sundar tilak bhurakamyank samananam
apharn tulsi das tras vihar vrinda kananam

radhe krishna radhe krishna krishna krishna radhe radhe
radhe shyam radhe shyam shyam shyam radhe radhe

Vinod Kumar

GOPAL GOKUL VALLABHI

dhin	na	-	dhin	dhin	na	-	dhin	na	-	dhin	dhin	na	-
1	2	3	4	5	6	7	1	2	3	4	5	6	7

flute: S--------------

.N S R S ---- S   S .N S
ae----------------- ae--------

S G R M*-----------------
ae-----------------------

M* P M* P----------- M G R S ------
ae---------------- ae-------------

dhin	na	-	dhin	dhin	na	-	dhin	na	-	dhin	dhin	na	-
1	2	3	4	5	6	7	1	2	3	4	5	6	7
													M*
													go
P	-	P	G	-	R	R	S	S	S	S	-	.N	.N
pa	-	l	go	-	ku	l	v	l	l	bhi	-	pri	y
.N	.P	.P	.N	-	S	S	G	R	G	R	-		
go	-	p	go	-	su	t	v	l	l	bhn	-		
												S	R
												ch	r
M*	-	M*	M*	-	M*	M*	P	-	M*	P	-	M*	P
na	-	r	vin	-	d	m	hn	-	bh	je	-	bh	j
S'	-	S'	N	D	N	P	P	N	M*	P	S		
ni	-	y	su	r	mu	ni	du	r	l	bhn	-		
												M*	P
												gh	n
S'	-	S'	S'	-	S'	S'	N	D	S'	N	N	P	-
shya	-	m	ka	-	m	a	ne	-	k	chh	vi	lo	-
M*	-	M*	P	-	D	D	N	D	N	P	-		
ka	-	bhi	ra	-	m	m	nau	-	h	rn	-		
												S	R
												kin	-

M*	M*	M*	M*	M*	M*	M*	P	-	P	P	-	M*	P
j	li	k	v	s	n	ki	sho	-	r	mu	-	r	ti
S'	-	S'	N	D	N	P	P	N	M*	P	S		
mu	-	l	gu	n	k	ru	na	-	k	ran	-		
												M*	P
												si	r
S'	-	S'	S'	-	S'	S'	N	D	S'	N	-	P	P
ke	-	ki	p	ch	chh	vi	lo	-	l	kun	-	d	l
M*	M*	M*	P	P	D	D	N	D	N	P	-		
a	ru	n	v	n	ru	h	lo	-	ch	nm	-		
												S	R
												gun	-
M*	-	M*	M*	-	M*	M*	P	-	P	P	P	M*	P
ja	-	v	tam	-	s	vi	chi	-	tr	s	b	an	g
S'	-	S'	N	D	N	P	P	N	M*	P	S		
dha	-	tu	bh	v	bh	y	mo	-	ch	nn	-		
												M*	P
												k	ch
S'	S'	S'	S'	-	S'	S'	N	D	S'	N	-	P	-
ku	ti	l	sun	-	d	r	ti	l	k	bhu	-	ra	-
M*	-	M*	P	-	D	D	N	D	N	P	-		
ka	-	m	ym	-	k	s	ma	-	n	nm	-		
												S	R
												a	p
M*	M*	M*	M*	M*	M*	-	P	-	P	P	-	M*	P
h	r	n	tu	l	si	-	da	-	s	tra	-	s	vi

Vinod Kumar

S'	-	S'	N	D	N	P	ᴾN	-	M*	P	S		
ha	-	r	vrin	-	da	-	ka	-	n	nn	-		
.N	.N	-	S	-	S	-	R	R	-	S	-	S	-
ra	dhe	-	kri	-	shna	-	ra	dhe	-	kri	-	shna	-
R	M*	M*	P	P	P	-	G	M	R	S	-	-	-
kri	sh	na	kri	sh	na	-	ra	dhe	ra	dhe	-	-	-
S	R	-	M*	-	-	M*	P	P	-	P	-	-	P
ra	dhe	-	shya	-	-	m	ra	dhe	-	shya	-	-	m
S'	-	N	P	-	-	P	G	M	R	S	-	-	-
shya	-	m	shya	-	-	m	ra	dhe	ra	dhe	-	-	-
P	P	-	S'	-	S'	-	R'	R'	-	S'	-	S'	-
ra	dhe	-	kri	-	shna	-	ra	dhe	-	kri	-	shna	-
S'	-	N	N	-	P	-	M*	M*	D	P	-	-	-
kri	sh	na	kri	sh	na	-	ra	dhe	ra	dhe	-	-	-
P	P	-	S'	-	-	S'	R'	R'	-	S'	-	-	S'
ra	dhe	-	shya	-	-	m	ra	dhe	-	shya	-	-	m
S'	-	N	N	-	-	P	M*	M*	D	P	-	-	-
shya	-	m	shya	-	-	m	ra	dhe	ra	dhe	-	-	-
.N	.N	-	S	-	S	-	R	R	-	S	-	S	-
ra	dhe	-	kri	-	shna	-	ra	dhe	-	kri	-	shna	-
R	M*	M*	P	P	P	-	G	M	R	S	-	-	-
kri	sh	na	kri	sh	na	-	ra	dhe	ra	dhe	-	-	-
.N	.N	-	S	-	-	S	R	R	-	S	-	-	S
ra	dhe	-	shya	-	-	m	ra	dhe	-	shya	-	-	m
R	M*	M*	P	-	-	P	G	M	R	S	-	-	-
shya	-	m	shya	-	-	m	ra	dhe	ra	dhe	-	-	-

15. HAM TO TUMSE RUTHE MOHAN

Krishna Bhajan
Lyrics: Goswami Bindu Ji
Maharaj
Taal: Kaharwa
https://youtu.be/8VjRH-mZeok

Music: Vinod Kumar
Singer: Vinod Kumar
Chord: MDS'   S=C#

jaan gaye ham chhalii prapanchi ho kapti ho jhuthe
ham to tumse ruthe mohan ham to tumse ruthe

pahle sharan bulaaya tha de de kar lobh anuthe
ab ik baar sharan dene me dikhlaye anguthe

sunte the dete ho sab sukh bhar bhar apne muthe
hamne shat shat 'Bindu' bahaaye diye na tukde juthe

HAM TO TUMSE RUTHE MOHAN

dha	ge	n	ti	n	ke	dhi	n	dha	ge	n	ti	n	ke	dhi	n
1	2	3	4	5	6	7	8	1	2	3	4	5	6	7	8
prelude: DDDD	PPPP	MMMM	PPPP	DDDD	PPPP	MMMM	D- S'-								
G	-	G	G	G	-	G	-	M	M	-	P	P	-	P	-
ja	-	n	g	ye	-	h	m	chh	li	-	pr	pn	-	chi	-
D	-	D	D	P	-	P	-	M	-	M	-	-	-	-	-
ho	-	k	p	ti	-	ho	-	jhu	-	the	-	-	-	-	-
D	S'	S'	-	S'	N	N	-	D	-	D	-	P	-	P	P
h	m	to	-	tu	m	se	-	ru	-	the	-	mo	-	h	n
P	D	D	-	P	P	P	-	M	-	M	-	-	-	-	-
h	m	to	-	tu	m	se	-	ru	-	the	-	-	-	-	-
interlude: DDDD	PPPP	MMMM	PPPP	DDDD	PPPP	MMMM	D S'-								
S'	S'	S'	-	S'	N	N	N	S'	-	S'	G'	R'	-	S'	-
p	h	le	-	sh	r	n	bu	la	-	ya	-	tha	-	de	-

Vinod Kumar

S'	-	S'	R'	S'	-	N	N	D	-	N	-	-	-	-	-
de	-	k	r	lo	-	bh	a	nu	-	the	-	-	-	-	-

D	S'	S'	S'	N	-	N	N	D	D	D	-	P	-	P	-
a	b	i	k	ba	-	r	sh	r	n	de	-	ne	-	me	-

P	D	D	-	P	-	P	-	M	-	M	-	-	-	-	-
di	kh	la	-	ye	-	an	-	gu	-	the	-	-	-	-	-

interlude: DDDD PPPP MMMM PPPP DDDD PPPP MMMM D S'-

S'	S'	S'	-	S'	-	N	-	S'	-	S'	G'	R'	R'	S'	S'
su	n	te	-	the	-	de	-	te	-	ho	-	s	b	su	kh

S'	-	S'	R'	S'	S'	N	-	D	-	N	-	-	-	-	-
bh	r	bh	r	a	p	ne	-	mu	-	the	-	-	-	-	-

D	S'	S'	-	S'	N	N	N	D	-	D	D	P	-	P	-
h	m	ne	-	sh	t	sh	t	bin	-	du	b	ha	-	ye	-

P	D	-	D	P	P	P	-	M	-	M	-	-	-	-	-
di	ye	-	n	tu	k	de	-	ju	-	the	-	-	-	-	-

G	-	G	G	G	-	G	-	M	M	-	P	P	-	P	-
ja	-	n	g	ye	-	h	m	chh	li	-	pr	pn	-	chi	-

D	-	D	D	P	-	P	-	M	-	M	-	-	-	-	-
ho	-	k	p	ti	-	ho	-	jhu	-	the	-	-	-	-	-

D	S'	S'	-	S'	N	N	-	D	-	D	-	P	-	P	P
h	m	to	-	tu	m	se	-	ru	-	the	-	mo	-	h	n

P	D	D	-	P	P	P	-	M	-	M	-	-	-	-	-
h	m	to	-	tu	m	se	-	ru	-	the	-	-	-	-	-

16. HAMARE SAATH SHRI RAGHUNATH

Sri Ram Bhajan
Lyrics: Brijesh
Taal: Rupak
https://youtu.be/zSioX0v5iPQ

Music: Prem Bhushan Ji
Singer: Prem Bhushan Ji
Chord: SGP   S=D#

hamaare saath shri raghunaath to kis baat ki chinta
sharan me rakh diya jab maath to kis baat ki chinta

kiya karte to hum din raat kyon bin baat ki chinta
tere swami -2 ko rahti hai tere har baat ki chinta
hamaare saath shri raghunaath to kis baat ki chinta

na khaane ki na piine ki na marne ki na jiine ki
rahe har swas -2 me bhagvan ke priya naam ki chinta
hamaare saath shri raghunaath to kis baat ki chinta

vibhishan ko abhaya var de kiya lankesh pal bhar me
unhin ka haan, unhin ka kar rahe gungaan to kis baat ki chinta
hamaare saath shri raghunaath to kis baat ki chinta

huyi 'brijesh' par kirpa banaaya das prabhu apna
unhin ke haath-2 me ab haath to kis baat ki chinta
hamaare saath shri raghunaath to kis baat ki chinta
sharan me rakh diya jab maath to kis baat ki chinta
to kis baat ki chinta, to kis baat ki chinta

Vinod Kumar

HAMARE SAATH SHRI RAGHUNATH

dhin	n	n	tin	n	tin	n	dhin	n	n	tin	n	tin	n
1	2	3	4	5	6	7	1	2	3	4	5	6	7
									S	S	-	S	R
									h	ma	-	re	-
G	-	G	G	-	G	G	M	-	M	G	-	R	R
sa	-	th	sari	-	r	ghu	na	-	th	to	-	ki	s
.N	-	.N	R	-	R	-	S	-	S	S	S	S	R
ba	-	t	ki	-	chin	-	ta	-	sh	r	n	me	-
G	G	G	G	-	G	G	M	-	M	G	-	R	R
r	kh	di	ya	-	j	b	ma	-	th	to	-	ki	s
.N	-	.N	R	-	R	-	S	-					
ba	-	t	ki	-	chin	-	ta	-					

interlude: play the first line of Antara.

dhin	n	n	tin	n	tin	n	dhin	n	n	tin	n	tin	n
1	2	3	4	5	6	7	1	2	3	4	5	6	7
									P	P	-	P	P
									ki	ya	-	k	r
N	D	D	N	N	N	N	S'	-	S'	S'	-	S'	S'
te	-	ho	tu	m	di	n	ra	-	t	kyun	-	bi	n
N	-	D	N	-	S'	-	N	P	S	S	-	S	R
ba	-	t	ki	-	chin	-	ta	-	te	re	-	swa	-
G	-	G	G	G	G	-	M	-	M	G	-	R	R
mi	-	ko	r	h	ti	-	hai	-	te	re	-	h	r
.N	-	.N	R	-	R	-	S	-					
ba	-	t	ki	-	chin	-	ta	-					
									P	P	-	P	-
									n	kha	-	ne	-
N	D	D	N	-	N	-	S'	-	S'	S'	-	S'	-
ki	-	n	pi	-	ne	-	ki	-	n	m	r	ne	-
N	-	D	N	-	S'	-	N	P	S	S	-	S	R
ki	-	n	Ji	-	ne	-	ki	-	r	he	-	h	r

G	-	G	G	-	G	G	M	-	M	G	-	R	R
shwa	-	s	me	-	bh	g	va	-	n	ke	-	pri	y
.N	-	.N	R	-	R	-	S	-					
na	-	m	ki	-	chin	-	ta	-					
							P			P	-	P	P
							vi			bhi	-	sh	n
N	D	D	N	N	N	N	S'	-	S'	S'	-	S'	-
ko	-	a	bh	y	v	r	de	-	di	ya	-	lan	-
N	-	D	N	N	S'	S'	N	P	S	S	-	S	R
ke	-	sh	pa	l	bh	r	me	-	u	nhi	-	ka	-
G	G	G	G	-	G	G	M	-	M	G	-	R	R
k	r	r	he	-	gu	n	ga	-	n	to	-	ki	s
.N	-	.N	R	-	R	-	S	-					
ba	-	t	ki	-	chin	-	ta	-					
							P			P	-	P	P
							hu			ii	-	bi	r
N	D	D	N	N	N	N	S'	-	S'	S'	-	S'	-
je	-	sh	p	r	ki	r	pa	-	b	na	-	ya	-
N	-	D	N	N	S'	S'	N	P	S	S	-	S	R
da	-	s	pr	bhu	a	p	na	-	u	nhi	-	ke	-
G	-	G	G	-	G	G	M	-	M	G	-	R	R
ha	-	th	me	-	a	b	ha	-	th	to	-	ki	s
.N	-	.N	R	-	R	-	S	-					
ba	-	t	ki	-	chin	-	ta	-					

Vinod Kumar

17.   HARI HAR JAPAA KAR

Lyrics: Goswami Sri Bindu Ji Maharaj   Music: Vinod Kumar
Taal: Daadra   Singer: Abhishek Bhama
       Chord: MDR'   S=C#
https://youtu.be/k29uHuDIKD0

sadaa apni rasnaa ko rasmaya banaakar
hari har hari har hari har japaa kar

is jap se kashton ka kam bhaar hogaa
is jap se papon ka pratikaar hogaa
is jap se nar tan ka shringaar hogaa
isi jap se tu prabhu ko sweekar hogaa
ye swason ki din raat maala banaakar
hari har hari har hari har japaa kar

is jap se aatmaa balvaan hogaa
is jap se kartavya ka dhyaan hogaa
is jap se santon ka sammaan hogaa
isi jap se santusht bhagwaan hogaa
akela ho ya saath sabko milaakar
hari har hari har hari har japaa kar

jo shraddha se is jap ko hai nitya gaataa
to iska yahi jap hai jeevan vidhaataa
yahi jap pita hai yahi jap hai maataa
yahi jap is jag me kalyaan daataa
isi ka koyi rup man me bithaakar
hari har hari har hari har japaa kar

ye jap tere man ko jab lalcha rahaa ho
vo rasikon ko is panth par laa rahaa ho
maza shri hari naam ka aa rahaa ho
hari hi hari har taraf chha rahaa ho
to kuchh prem ke 'bindu' drig se bahaakar
hari har hari har hari har japaa kar

HARI HAR JAPAA KAR

dha 1	dhi 2	na 3	dha 4	tu 5	na 6	dha 1	dhi 2	na 3	dha 4	tu 5	na 6
prelude:											
S'	S'	S'	-	S'	-	N	N	N	-	N	-
D	D	P	-	-	N	D	-	-	-	-	-
D	D	D	-	D	-	P	P	P	-	P	-
G	G	G	-	-	P	M	-	-	-	-	
											M
											s
M	R'	R'	R'	R'	-	S'	R'	S'	N	-	N
da	-	a	p	ni	-	r	s	na	-	-	ko
S'	R'	S'	-	-	N	D	-	P	-	-	G
r	s	may	-	-	b	na	-	kr	-	-	h
G	P	P	-	-	P	P	D	D	-	-	D
ri	-	hr	-	-	h	ri	-	hr	-	-	h
N	D	P	-	-	M	M	-	M	-	-	
ri	-	hr	-	-	j	pa	-	kr	-	-	
S'	S'	S'	-	S'	-	N	N	N	-	N	-
D	D	P	-	-	N	D	-	-	-	-	-
D	D	D	-	D	-	P	P	P	-	P	-
G	G	G	-	-	P	M	-	-	-	-	
G	G	G	G	G	-	M	-	M	-	-	M
i	s	j	p	se	-	k	-	shto	-	-	ka
P	D	P	-	-	M	M	-	M	-	-	M
k	m	bha	-	-	r	ho	-	ga	-	-	i
G	-	G	G	G	-	M	-	M	-	-	M
si	-	j	p	se	-	pa	-	po	-	-	ka

Vinod Kumar

P	D	P	-	-	M	M	-	M	-	-	M
pr	ti	ka	-	-	r	ho	-	ga	-	-	i
D	-	D	D	D	-	N̲	N̲	N̲	-	-	N̲
si	-	j	p	se	-	n	r	tn	-	-	ka
N̲	-	N̲	-	-	D	S'	-	N̲	-	-	N̲
shrin	-	ga	-	-	r	ho	-	ga	-	-	i
S'	G̲'	R'	S'	N̲	-	D	-	P	P	P	-
si	-	j	p	se	-	tu	-	pr	bhu	ko	-
N̲	D	P	-	-	M	M	-	M	-	-	M
swi	-	ka	-	-	r	ho	-	ga	-	-	ye
M	R'	R'	-	-	R'	S'	R'	S'	N̲	-	N̲
shwa	-	so	-	-	ki	di	n	ra	-	-	t
S'	R'	S'	-	-	N̲	D	-	P	-	-	G
ma	-	la	-	-	b	na	-	kr	-		h
G	P	P	-	-	P	P	D	D	-	-	D
ri	-	hr	-	-	h	ri	-	hr	-	-	h
N̲	D	P	-	-	M	M	-	M	-	-	M
ri	-	hr	-	-	j	pa	-	kr	-	-	s
M	R'	R'	R'	R'	-	S'	R'	S'	N̲	-	N̲
da	-	a	p	ni	-	r	s	na	-	-	ko
S'	R'	S'	-	-	N̲	D	-	P	-	-	G
r	s	may	-	-	b	na	-	kr	-	-	h
G	P	P	-	-	P	P	D	D	-	-	D
ri	-	hr	-	-	h	ri	-	hr	-	-	h
N̲	D	P	-	-	M	M	-	M	-	-	
ri	-	hr	-	-	j	pa	-	kr	-	-	

18. HE MURALI MANOHAR GOPALA

Krishna Bhajan

Lyrics: Jagjit Singh

Taal: Kaharwa

https://youtu.be/BaTf1NdBqQo

Music: Jagjit Singh

Singer: Jagjit Singh

Chord: SGP   S=C#

he murali manohar   gopala -2
murali manohar   gopala -2

govind radhe gopala -2
murli manohar   gopala -2

he murali manohar   gopala -2
govind ra-dhe-   go-pa-la- -2

he murali manohar   gopala -2
murali manohar   gopala -2

pandri- data jay hari   vitthala- -2
jay govrdhan   gopala -2
murali manohar   gopala -2

HE MURALI MANOHAR GOPALA

dha	ge	na	ti	n	ke	dhin	n	dha	ge	na	ti	n	ke	dhin	n
1	2	3	4	5	6	7	8	1	2	3	4	5	6	7	8

R RRG   MGS.D   SSS
he murali manohar   gopala

RRG   MGS.D   SSS
murali manohar   gopala

MMM   MM   MGMPPG
govind radhe gopala

PPM MGS.D   SSS
murli manohar   gopala

R RR<u>G</u>   M<u>GS</u>.<u>D</u>   SSS
he murali manohar   gopala

PPP   PMP<u>N</u>   <u>D</u>-PMP<u>G</u>
govind ra-dhe-   go-pa-la-

<u>D</u>   <u>D</u>DP M<u>GS</u>.<u>D</u>   SSS
he murali manohar   gopala

RR<u>G</u>   M<u>GS</u>.<u>D</u>   SSS
murali manohar   gopala

<u>G</u>MPS' S'S' <u>N</u> S'S'   <u>N</u>S'<u>D</u>P
pandri- data jay hari   vitthala

<u>D</u>   <u>D</u>M<u>GS</u>.<u>D</u>   SSS
jay govrdhan   gopala

RR<u>G</u>   M<u>GS</u>.<u>D</u>   SSS
murali manohar   gopala

19. HO RASIYA MAIN TO SHARAN

Krishna Bhajan
Taal: Bhajani

Music: Jagjit Singh
Singer: Jagjit Singh
Chord: SGP   S=C

https://youtu.be/uwvHtlCpET8

ho rasiya main to sharan tihari
nahin saadhn bal vachan chaturi, ek bharoso girdhari

main ati deen tumhri sharan me, nath n dijyo visaar
aapno jani sanbhalo priitam, prem sakhi balihari

radhe krishna radhe krishna, krishna krishna radhe radhe
radhe shyam radhe shyam, shyam shyam radhe radhe

HO RASIYA MAIN TO SHARAN

Intro:
P DGM—MGR G M GGR RSS
ho rsiya------- main to Sharan tihari

dhin-n 1	dhin 2	-dhi 3	na- 4	tin- 5	ntin 6	-ti 7	na- 8	dhin-n 1	dhin 2	-dhi 3	na- 4	tin- 5	ntin 6	-ti 7	na- 8
								P	-			-	D	-	G
								ho	-			-	r	-	si
M	-	-	-	M	G	R	-	-	-	G	-	M	P	-	-
ya	-	-	-	-	-	-	-	-	-	main	-	-	to	-	-
-	-	G	G	-	R	-	R	S	-	-	-	S	-	-	-
-	-	sh	r	-	n	-	ti	ha	-	-	-	ri	-	-	-
-	-	P	-	G	P	-	D	S'	-	-	-	-	-	-	-
-	-	ho	-	-	r	-	si	ya	-	-	-	-	-	-	-
-	-	-	-	N	-	P	D	S'	-	N	-	M	P	G	R
-	-	-	-	-	-	-	-	-	-	-	-	-	-	-	-
-	-	G	M	-	P	M	-	-	-	G	G	-	R	-	R
-	-	main	-	-	to	-	-	-	-	sh	r	-	n	-	ti
S	-	-	-	S	-	-	-	-	-	P	-	-	D	-	G
ha	-	-	-	ri	-	-	-	-	-	o	-	-	r	-	si
M	-	-	-	M	G	R	-	-	-	G	-	-	M	-	-
ya	-	-	-	-	-	-	-	-	-	main	-	-	to	-	-
-	-	G	G	-	R	-	R	S	-	-	-	S	-	-	-
-	-	sh	r	-	n	-	ti	ha	-	-	-	ri	-	-	-
-	-	P	-	G	P	-	D	S'	-	-	NS'	PD	MP	G	R
-	-	ho	-	-	r	-	si	ya	-	-	-	-	-	-	-
-	-	G	M	-	P	M	-	-	-	G	G	-	R	-	R
-	-	main	-	-	to	-	-	-	-	sh	r	-	n	-	ti
S	-	-	-	S	-	-	-	-	-						
ha	-	-	-	ri	-	-	-	-	-						

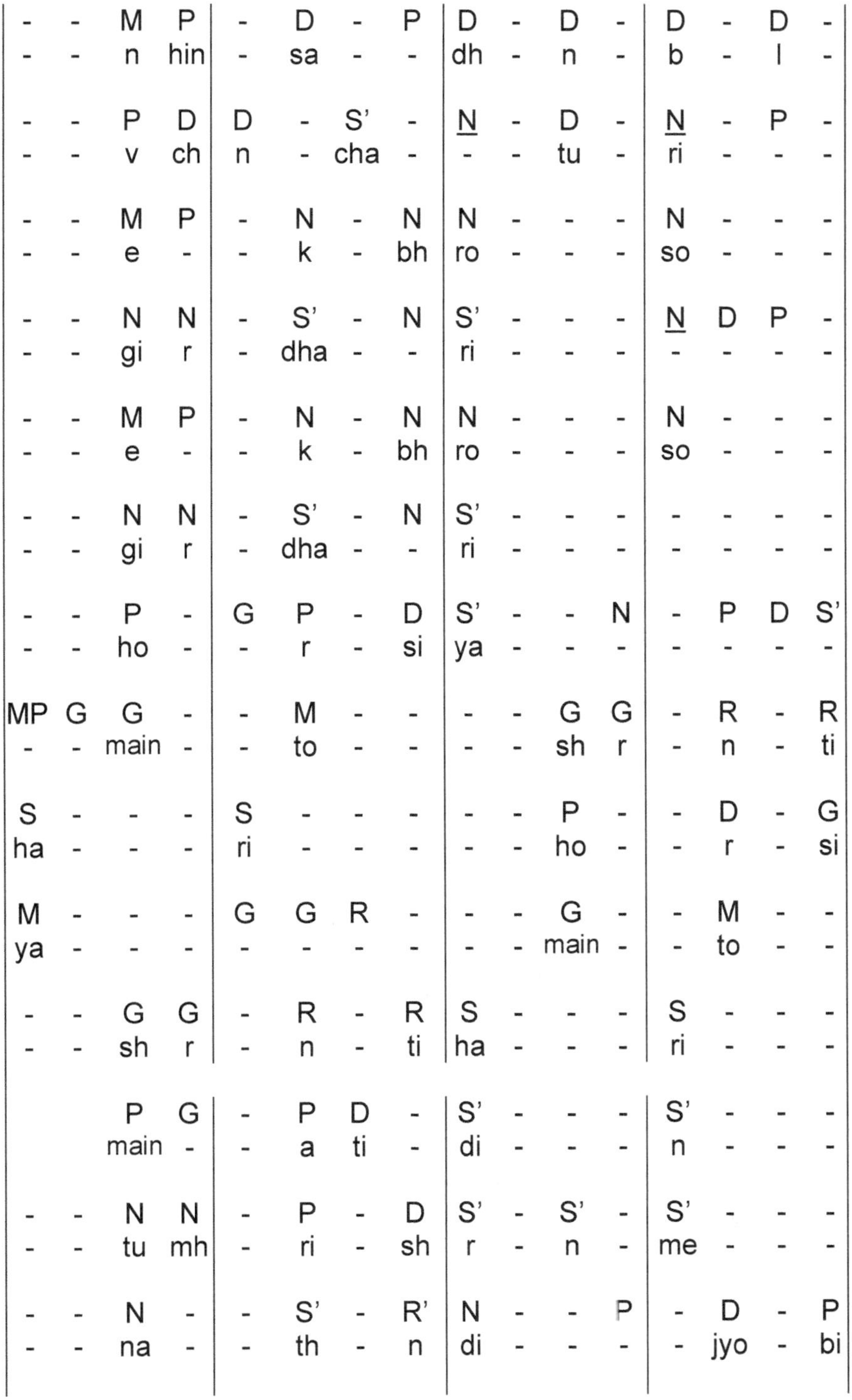

Vinod Kumar

-	-	M	P	-	D	-	P	D	-	D	-	D	-	D	-
-	-	n	hin	-	sa	-	-	dh	-	n	-	b	-	l	-
-	-	P	D	D	-	S'	-	N	-	D	-	N	-	P	-
-	-	v	ch	n	-	cha	-	-	-	tu	-	ri	-	-	-
-	-	M	P	-	N	-	N	N	-	-	-	N	-	-	-
-	-	e	-	-	k	-	bh	ro	-	-	-	so	-	-	-
-	-	N	N	-	S'	-	N	S'	-	-	-	N	D	P	-
-	-	gi	r	-	dha	-	-	ri	-	-	-	-	-	-	-
-	-	M	P	-	N	-	N	N	-	-	-	N	-	-	-
-	-	e	-	-	k	-	bh	ro	-	-	-	so	-	-	-
-	-	N	N	-	S'	-	N	S'	-	-	-	-	-	-	-
-	-	gi	r	-	dha	-	-	ri	-	-	-	-	-	-	-
-	-	P	-	G	P	-	D	S'	-	-	N	-	P	D	S'
-	-	ho	-	-	r	-	si	ya	-	-	-	-	-	-	-
MP	G	G	-	-	M	-	-	-	-	G	G	-	R	-	R
-	-	main	-	-	to	-	-	-	-	sh	r	-	n	-	ti
S	-	-	-	S	-	-	-	-	-	P	-	-	D	-	G
ha	-	-	-	ri	-	-	-	-	-	ho	-	-	r	-	si
M	-	-	-	G	G	R	-	-	-	G	-	-	M	-	-
ya	-	-	-	-	-	-	-	-	-	main	-	-	to	-	-
-	-	G	G	-	R	-	R	S	-	-	-	S	-	-	-
-	-	sh	r	-	n	-	ti	ha	-	-	-	ri	-	-	-
		P	G	-	P	D	-	S'	-	-	-	S'	-	-	-
		main	-	-	a	ti	-	di	-	-	-	n	-	-	-
-	-	N	N	-	P	-	D	S'	-	S'	-	S'	-	-	-
-	-	tu	mh	-	ri	-	sh	r	-	n	-	me	-	-	-
-	-	N	-	-	S'	-	R'	N	-	-	P	-	D	-	P
-	-	na	-	-	th	-	n	di	-	-	-	-	jyo	-	bi

P	-	-	-	P	-	-	-	-	-	N	-	-	S'	-	R'
sa	-	-	-	ri	-	-	-	-	-	na	-	-	th	-	n
N	-	-	P	-	D	-	P	M	-	-	-	G	-	-	G
di	-	-	-	-	jyo	-	bi	sa	-	-	-	ri	-	-	-
S	-	P	-	G	P	-	D	S'	-	-					
-	-	ho	-	-	r	-	si	ya	-	-					
		P	G	-	P	D	-	S'	-	-	-	S'	-	-	-
		a	p	-	nau	-	-	ja	-	-	-	ni	-	-	-
-	-	S'	S'	-	P	D	-	S'	-	-	-	S'	-	S'	-
-	-	sn	bha	-	lo	-	-	prii	-	-	-	t	-	m	-
-	-	N	-	-	S'	-	R'	S'	-	-	-	-	N	-	D
-	-	pre	-	-	m	-	s	khi	-	-	-	-	b	-	li
N	-	P	-	P	-	-	-	-	-	N	-	-	S'	-	R'
ha	-	-	-	ri	-	-	-	-	-	pre	-	-	m	-	s
D	-	P	-	-	D	-	P	M	-	-	-	G	-	-	R
khi	-	-	-	-	b	-	li	ha	-	-	-	ri	-	-	-
S	-														
-	-														

P   DGM—MGR   G M GGR RSS
ho rasiya-------   main to sharan tihari

PG PDS'---- N- PDS'—N—PDMPG-R-
ho rasiya ------------------------------

  G   M GGR RSS
main to sharan tihari

P   DGM- ^{P}G-R-- G M GGR RSS
ho rasiya -------   main to sharan tihari

PG PDS'---R'—^{N}PDS'- N-DPMGR
ho rasiya -------------------------

Vinod Kumar

G   M GGR   RSS
main to sharan tihari

| - - G - | G   R   - R | S - S - | S - S - |
| - - ra - | dhe kri - shna | ra - dhe - | kri - shna - |

| - - S - | R   S - .N | .N - S - | S - R - |
| - - kri - | shna kri - shna | ra - dhe - | ra - dhe - |

| - - R - | P   P   - P | M - G - | R - - - |
| - - ra - | dhe shya - m | ra - dhe - | shya - m - |

| - - M   - | G R   - R | S - S - | S - S - |
| - - shya - | m shya - m | ra - dhe - | ra - dhe - |

| - - P - | P   P   - P | P - D - | P - M - |
| - - ra - | dhe kri - shna | ra - dhe - | kri - shna - |

| - - P - | D   N - S' | S' - N - | D - P - |
| - - kri - | shna kri - shna | ra - dhe - | ra - dhe - |

| - - P - | P   P   - P | P - D - | P - M - |
| - - ra - | dhe shya - m | ra - dhe - | shya - m - |

| - - P   - | D N   - S' | S' - N - | D - P - |
| - - shya - | m shya - m | ra - dhe - | ra - dhe - |

| - - S' - | S' S' - S' | S' - R' - | S' - N - |
| - - ra - | dhe kri - shna | ra - dhe - | kri - shna - |

| - - S' - | S'   R' - G' | R' - G' - | R' - S' - |
| - - kri - | shna kri - shna | ra - dhe - | ra - dhe - |

| - - S' - | S' S' - S' | S' - R' - | S' - N - |
| - - ra - | dhe shya - m | ra - dhe - | shya - m - |

| - - S' - | S' R' - G' | R' - G' - | R' - S' - |
| - - shya - | m shya - m | ra - dhe - | ra - dhe - |

| - - G - | G   R   - R | S - S - | S - S - |
| - - ra - | dhe kri - shna | ra - dhe - | kri - shna - |

-	-	S	-	R	S	-	.N	.N	-	S	-	S	-	R	-
-	-	kri	-	shna	kri	-	shna	ra	-	dhe	-	ra	-	dhe	-
-	-	R	-	P	P	-	P	M	-	G	-	R	-	-	-
-	-	ra	-	dhe	shya	-	m	ra	-	dhe	-	shya	-	m	-
-	-	M	-	G	R	-	R	S	-	S	-	S	-	S	-
-	-	shya	-	m	shya	-	m	ra	-	dhe	-	ra	-	dhe	-

20. JAY GAURI SHANKARA

Shiv Bhajan   Raag: Aabheri or Bhimpalasi
Taal: Kaharwa   Chord: SGP   S=.G#

mandara maal dhara jay gauri shankaraa
har haraa paahi trinetra
gangadhar bimbadhar chandramauli shankaraa
gangadhar bimbadhar chandramauli shankaraa
mandara maal dhara jay gauri shankaraa

vaamdev mahaadev shiv shiv shiv shankaraa
satya dharm shaanti prem satya om shankaraa
satya dharm shaanti prem satya om shankaraa
mandara maal dhara jay gauri shankaraa

Vinod Kumar

JAY GAURI SHANKARA

dha	ge	na	ti	n	ke	dhin	n	dha	ge	na	ti	n	ke	dhin	n
1	2	3	4	5	6	7	8	1	2	3	4	5	6	7	8

SGM   PN MP M PM GRG
mandara maal dhara jay gauri shankaraa

M   PN   NS' R'N NS'--- NDP
har haraa paahi trinetra-----------

S'S'S'S'   NDPP   MPPM   GRG
gangadhar bimbadhar chandramauli shankaraa

S'S'R'R' NDPP   MPPM   GRG
gangadhar bimbadhar chandramauli shankaraa

S G M ND MP M PP GRG
mandara maal dhara jay gauri shankaraa

MPNN   NNS'S' NS' S'R' R'S' NS'S'
vaamdev mahaadev shiv shiv   shiv shankaraa

NS' S'S' ND   PM MP PM GRG
satya dharm shaanti prem satya om shankaraa

NS' R'S' ND   PM MP NP GRG
satya dharm shaanti prem satya om shankaraa

21. JAY JAY RAMA

Ram Bhajan
Taal: Kaharwa

Chord: S<u>G</u>P   S=.G
Raag: Bhimpalasi

jay jay rama jay raghurama, dashrath nandan raja rama
abhaya pradayak aanand dayak, tribhuvan mohan sita rama
daanv bhanjan diin uddhaaran, prem sagra jay sri rama

JAY JAY RAMA

dha	ge	n	ti	n	ke	dhi	n	dha	ge	n	ti	n	ke	dhi	n
1	2	3	4	5	6	7	8	1	2	3	4	5	6	7	8
prelude: S<u>G</u>P															
-	-	P	<u>N</u>	-	S'	R'	-	<u>G'</u>	-	R'	-	S'	-	<u>N</u>	-
-	-	j	y	-	j	y	-	ra	-	-	-	ma	-	-	-
-	-	P	<u>N</u>	-	S'	<u>N</u>	-	R'	-	-	-	S'	<u>N</u>	P	-
-	-	j	y	-	r	ghu	-	ra	-	-	-	ma	-	-	-
-	-	P	S'	-	<u>N</u>	D	-	M	-	<u>G</u>	-	M	P	P	-
-	-	d	sh	-	r	th	-	nn	-	-	-	d	-	n	-
<u>G</u>	-	M	-	-	R	-	.<u>N</u>	S	-	-	-	S	-	-	-
-	-	ra	-	-	ja	-	-	ra	-	-	-	ma	-	-	-
-	-	<u>G</u>	<u>G</u>	-	.<u>N</u>	-	S	M	-	M	-	M	-	M	-
-	-	a	bh	-	y	-	pr	da	-	-	-	y	-	k	-
<u>G</u>	-	P	-	-	<u>G</u>	-	M	P	-	<u>N</u>	-	D	-	D	-
-	-	aa	-	-	nn	-	d	da	-	-	-	y	-	k	-
P	-	P	<u>N</u>	-	P	-	M	<u>N</u>	-	-	-	<u>N</u>	-	<u>N</u>	-
-	-	tri	bu	-	v	-	n	mo	-	-	-	h	-	n	-
-	-	P<u>N</u> S'R'		-	<u>N</u>	-	P	S'	-	-	-	S'	-	-	-
-	-	si-	--	-	ta	-	-	ra	-	-	-	ma	-	-	-
-	-	<u>G'</u>	-	-	G'	-	R'	<u>G'</u>	-	-	-	<u>G'</u>	-	<u>G'</u>	-
-	-	da	-	-	n	-	v	bhn	-	-	-	j	-	n	-

Vinod Kumar

-	-	R'	-	-	N	-	-	S'	R'	G'	-	R'	-	R'	-
-	-	di	-	-	nau	-	-	ddha	-	-	-	r	-	n	-
-	-	G'	-	-	G'	-	R'	M'	-	-	-	G'	-	G'	-
-	-	da	-	-	n	-	v	bhn	-	-	-	j	-	n	-
-	-	R'	-	-	N	-	-	S'	R'	G'	-	R'	-	R'	-
-	-	di	-	-	nau	-	-	ddha	-	-	-	r	-	n	-
-	-	N	-	N	-	S'	-	-	-	R'	-	S'	R'	G'	-
-	-	pre	-	m	-	sa	-	-	-	g	-	ra	-	-	-
-	-	R'	-	-	N	-	-	S'	-	-	-	S'	-	-	-
-	-	j	y	-	sri	-	-	ra	-	-	-	ma	-	-	-
-	-	N	-	N	-	S'	-	-	-	R'	-	S'	R'	G'	-
-	-	pre	-	m	-	sa	-	-	-	g	-	ra	-	-	-
-	-	R'	-	-	N	-	-	R'	-	-	-	S'	-	-	-
-	-	j	y	-	sri	-	-	ra	-	-	-	ma	-	-	-
-	-	P	N	-	S'	R'	-	G'	-	R'	-	S'	-	N	-
-	-	j	y	-	j	y	-	ra	-	-	-	ma	-	-	-
-	-	P	N	-	S'	N	-	R'	-	-	-	S'	N	P	-
-	-	j	y	-	r	ghu	-	ra	-	-	-	ma	-	-	-
-	-	P	S'	-	N	D	-	M	-	G	-	M	P	P	-
-	-	d	sh	-	r	th	-	nn	-	-	-	d	-	n	-
G	-	M	-	-	R	-	.N	S	-	-	-	S	-	-	-
-	-	ra	-	-	ja	-	-	ra	-	-	-	ma	-	-	-

22. JAY JAY HANUMAAN

Sri Hanuman Bhajan
Taal: Kaharwa

Raag: Bhimpalasi
Chord: S<u>G</u>P   S=.A

jay jay hanuman jay hanuman
jay jay hanuman jay hanuman
maruti raya jay hanuman
mahanubhava jay hanuman
vayu kumara jay hanuman
vaanar viiraa jay hanuman
anjani putra jay hanuman
ati balvnta jay hanuman
sri ram duta jay hanuman
sri ram bhakta jay hanuman

JAY JAY HANUMAAN

dha	ge	n	ti	n	ke	dhi	n	dha	ge	n	ti	n	ke	dhi	n
1	2	3	4	5	6	7	8	1	2	3	4	5	6	7	8
P	-	S'	-	<u>N</u>	D	P	-	M	P	<u>G</u>	M	P	-	-	-
jai	-	jai	-	h	nu	ma	-n	jai	-	h	nu	ma	-	-	-n
M	-	M	<u>G</u>	M	P	P	-	<u>G</u>	-	R	<u>G</u>	S	-	-	-
jai	-	jai	-	h	nu	ma	-n	jai	-	h	nu	ma	-	-	-n
P	-	P	P	M	P	<u>G</u>	M	P	-	<u>N</u>	<u>N</u>	S'	-	-	-
ma	-	ru	ti	ra	-	ya	-	jai	-	h	nu	ma	-	-	-n
P	P	<u>N</u>	S'	<u>G</u>'	-	<u>G</u>'	-	R'	-	<u>N</u>	R'	R'	S'	-	-
m	ha	-	nu	bha	-	va	-	jai	-	h	nu	ma	-	-	-n
S'	-	S'	S'	<u>N</u>	-	D	-	P	-	<u>G</u>	M	P	-	-	-
va	-	yu	ku	ma	-	ra	-	jai	-	h	nu	ma	-	-	-n
M	-	M	<u>G</u>	M	P	P	-	<u>G</u>	-	R	<u>G</u>	S	-	-	-
va	-	n	r	vii	-	ra	-	jai	-	h	nu	ma	-	-	-n

Vinod Kumar

P	-	P	P	M	P	G	M	P	-	N	N	S'	-	-	-
an	-	j	ni	pu	-	tra	-	jai	-	h	nu	ma	-	-	-n
N	N	N	N	S'	G'	G'	-	R'	-	N	R'	R'	S'	-	-
a	ti	b	l	vn	-	ta	-	jai	-	h	nu	ma	-	-	-n
S'	-	S'	S'	N	-	D	P	P	-	G	M	P	-	-	-
sri	-	ra	-m	du	-	ta	-	jai	-	h	nu	ma	-	-	-n
M	-	M	G	M	P	P	-	G	-	R	G	S	-	-	-
sri	-	ra	-m	bh	k	ta	-	jai	-	h	nu	ma	-	-	-n
P	-	S'	-	N	D	P	-	M	P	G	M	P	-	-	-
jai	-	jai	-	h	nu	ma	-n	jai	-	h	nu	ma	-	-	-n
M	-	M	G	M	P	P	-	G	-	R	G	S	-	-	-
jai	-	jai	-	h	nu	ma	-n	jai	-	h	nu	ma	-	-	-n

23.   KYA BHAROSA HAI IS ZINDAGI KA

Taal: Kaharwa   Chord: SGP   S=C#

https://youtu.be/vLTZt0Ar0v4

kya bharosa hai is zindagi ka, sath deti nahin yeh kisi ka

saans ruk jaayegi chalte chalte, shamma bujh jaayegi jalte jalte
dam nikal jaayega raushani ka, kya bharosa hai is zindagi ka

ham rahein na mohobbat rahegi, daastaan apni duniya kahegi
naam rah jayega aadmi ka, kya bharosa hai is zindagi ka

duniya hai ik haqeeqat purani, chalte rahna hai uski ravaani
farz pura karo bandagi ka, kya bharosa hai is zindagi ka

KYA BHAROSA HAI IS ZINDAGI KA

dha	ge	na	ti	n	ke	dhin	n	dha	ge	na	ti	n	ke	dhin	n
1	2	3	4	5	6	7	8	1	2	3	4	5	6	7	8

prelude :
S'R'S' NS'R' G'–R'– NS'R'S'– S'R'S' NS'R' G'–R'– NS'R'S'–
P'D'P'M' M'P'M'G' G'M'G'R'R'S'- P'D'P'M' M'P'M'G'
G'M'G'R'R'S'-
S'R'S' NS'R' G'–R'– NS'R'S'– S'R'S' NS'R' G'–R'– NS'R'S'–

S RGM M G GRS S
kya bharosa hai is zindagi ka

PP DS' ND P MG M
sath deti nahin yeh kisi ka

music:
PPP P PDP S'– ND- PM- GM-
RRR P-M M-G G-R R-S S-

antra
GM P PPP ND PP (MG)
saans ruk jaayegi chalte chalte

GM P PPP ND PP (MG)
shamma bujh jaayegi jalte jalte

P PDS' S'S'N DPG M
dam nikal jaayega raushani ka

S RGM M G GRS S
kya bharosa hai is zindagi ka

interlude:
G'G' R'R' R'R' S'S'
D – N – N – S' - - (R' S' N)
NS' G'G' G' – M'G'R'S'
NS' R'S' S' - - -

antra
G   MP   P   PPDN   DPP   (M)
ham rahein na mohobbat rahegi

GMP   PP   PDN   DPP (M)
daastaan apni duniya kahegi

PP   DS' S'S'N   DPG   M
naam rah jayega aadmi ka

S   RGM   M G GRS   S
kya bharosa hai is zindagi ka

antra:
GMP   P   P   PDN   DPP (M)
duniya hai ik haqeeqat purani

GM   PP   P   PDN   DPP (M)
chalte rahna hai uski ravaani

PP   DS' ND   PMG   M
farz pura karo bandagi ka

S   RGM   M G GRS   S
kya bharosa hai is zindagi ka

24. LADDU JAISA HAI LADDU GOPAL

Krishna Bhajan
Lyrics: Sri Kewal Krishna
'Madhup'
Taal: Kaharwa of Tisr Jaati
https://youtu.be/hfWqIHWIAKs

Singer: Mohan Das (Tinu Singh)
Chord: SGP   MDS'   S=.A#

nand lal ki pranan pyara mata yashoda laal
madhup gopi gwalon ka ye thakur laddu gopal
laddu gopal ki jay

laddu jaisa laddu jaisa
laddu jaisa hai laddu gopal mujhe bada pyara lage -2
nand yashoda ka ye baal (lal) mujhe bada pyara lage -2

golmatol mera laddu gopala -2
bada bhola bhala lage jag se nirala -2
laddu gopala jag se nirala
bada komal -3 hai rup rasal mujhe bada pyara lage

dudh dahi chhachh se ise nahlaun -2
maakhan misri ka bhog lagaun -2
ise nahlaun bhog lagaaun
bada natkhat -3 hai gokul ka gwal mujhe bada pyara lage

shish mukut pitambar pahnaun -2
nazar na lage kala tika lagaun -2
mukut pahnaun tika lagaun
radha naam ki pahnaun maal mujhe bada pyara lage

radha ka chitchor saanvla slona -2
khele khilauno se brij ka khilauna -2
saanvla slauna brij ka khilauna
khel khele madhup ye kamaal mujhe bada pyara lage

Vinod Kumar

LADDU JAISA HAI LADDU GOPAL

dha	dhi	na	dha	tu	na	dha	dhi	na	dha	tu	na
1	2	3	4	5	6	1	2	3	4	5	6
one			Two			Three			four		

```
PM   MM   M    PMM  MM   DD   DMD  PP
nand laal ki   prann pyara mata yshoda lal

PDD      DD   MDPM  G  R  GG   GRS  RS-
madhup   gopi gwa-lo- ka ye thakur laddu gopal

NS'   NS'   S'   S' (Chord-MDS')
laddu gopal ki   jay
```

1	2	3	4	5	6	1	2	3	4	5	6
									S	R	-
									l	ddu	-
R	-	G	-	-	-	-	-	-	P	M*	-
jai	-	sa	-	-	-	-	-	-	l	ddu	-
R	-	G	-	-	-	-	-	-	S	R	-
jai	-	sa	-	-	-	-	-	-	l	ddu	-
R	-	G	-	G	-	G	-	M	-	G	-
jai	-	sa	-	hai	-	l	-	ddu	-	go	-
R	G	R	-	-	-	.N	.N	-	R	R	-
pa	-	-	l	-	-	mu	jhe	-	b	da	-
G	-	R	-	S	-	S	-	-	S	R	-
pya	-	ra	-	l	-	ge	-	-	nn	d	-
R	G	-	G	-	-	-	-	-	P	M*	-
y	sho	-	da	-	-	-	-	-	nn	d	-
R	G	-	G	-	-	-	-	-	S	R	-
y	sho	-	da	-	-	-	-	-	nn	d	-
R	G	-	G	-	-	G	-	P	M	G	-
y	sho	-	da	-	-	ka	-	-	ye	-	-

R	G	R	-	-	-	.N	.N	-	R	R	-
la	-	-	l	-	-	mu	jhe	-	b	da	-
G	-	R	-	S	-	S	-	-			
pya	-	ra	-	l	-	ge	-	-			

interlude: G M P MG R   R G M GR S x2

S	-	G	-	M		P	-	-	P	P	-
go	-	l	-	m	-	to	-	l	me	ra	-
M*	-	P	-	P	-	M	-	-	P	G	-
l	-	ddu	-	go	-	pa	-	-	la	-	-
S	S	-	G	M	-	P	P	-	P	P	-
b	da	-	bho	la	-	bha	la	-	l	ge	-
M*	M*	P	-	D	-	M	-	-	P	G	-
j	g	se	-	ni	-	ra	-	-	la	-	-
P	-	P	-	D	-	M	-	-	G	-	-
l	-	ddu	-	go	-	pa	-	-	la	-	-
P	P	P	-	D	-	M	-	-	G	-	-
j	g	se	-	ni	-	ra	-	-	la	-	-
-	-	-	S	R	-	G	-	G	-	-	-
			b	da	-	ko	-	m	l		
-	-	-	P	M*	-	R	-	G	-	-	-
-	-	-	b	da	-	ko	-	m	l		
-	-	-	S	R	-	G	-	G	-	G	-
-	-	-	b	da	-	ko	-	m	l	hai	-
G	P	-	M	-	G	R	G	R	-	-	-
ru	-	-	p	-	r	sa	-	-	-	l	-
.N	.N	-	R	R	-	G	-	R	-	S	-
mu	jhe	-	b	da	-	pya	-	ra	-	l	-
S	-	-									
ge	-	-									

Vinod Kumar

interlude: G M P MG R   R G M GR S *x2*

SS   GM   PP   P M*M*   PPM-PG
dudh dahi chhachh se ise   nahlaun

S-GM   PP   P   M*-P   PM-PG
maakhan misri ka   bhog   lagaun

M*M*   PPM-G   M*-P   PM-G   MPGMRGS
ise   nahlaun   bhog   lagaaun   music

SR   G- G-   PM* R-G-
bada natkhat   bada natkhat

SR   G-G-   G G-M- G RGR .N.N   RR   GR   SS
bada natkhat hai gokul ka   gwal   mujhe bada pyara   lage

Iddu jaisa hai Iddu gopal mujhe bda pyara....

SG   MPP   P M* P   PM-G
shish mukut pitambar pahnaun

SSG M PP   PP   M*-P   PM-PG
nazar na lage kala   tika   lagaun

M*M*P P-M-G   M*-P P M-G   MPGMRGS
mukut   pahnaun   tika   lagaun   music

SR   GG G PM* RGG G
radha nam ki radha na-m ki

SR   GG G GPMG RGR .N.N RR   GR   SS
radha naam ki pahnaun maal mujhe bada pyara lage

Iddu jaiS hai Iddu gopal mujhe bda pyara...

SG   M PP P   M*M*P   PM-PG
radha ka chitchor saanvla   slona

S-G M PP   P   M*   P   PM-P G
khele khilauno se brij   ka   khilauna

```
M*M*P   PM-G   M*M*  P   PM-G   MPGMRGS
saanvla slauna  brij   ka  khilauna music

SR   G- G-    PM*  R-G-
khel khe-le-   khel  khe-le-

SR   G-G-  GGP  M-  G RGR  .N.N  RR   GR   SS
khel khele  madhup ye kamaal   mujhe bada pyara lage

Iddu jaisa hai Iddu gopal mujhe bda pyara...
```

25. MERA MAN PANCHHI YE CHAHE

Krishna Bhajan
Taal: Kaharwa/Bhajani

Singer: Aacharya Mukesh
Bhardwaj Ji Maharaj
Chord: GDS'   S=C#

https://youtu.be/G2Vo9HgtpwY

ho ho ho ho ho he he he he
mera man pnchhi ye chahe ud vrndavan jaun,
brij ki un paavan galiyon me radhe radhe gaun,
main radhe radhe gaun main shyama shyama gaun,
mera man pnchhi ye....

mor mukut pitambar sohe gal vaijanti mala
thodi pe mere thakur ke hira damke aala
banke bihari girdhari koii kahe nand ko lala
ya hi chhvi pe balihari sab brij ke gopi gwala
yugal charan chhvi nirkhi nirkhi ho... nij jiivn safal banaun
brij ki un paavan galiyon me radhe radhe gaun,
main radhe radhe gaun main shyama shyama gaun,

seva kunj nidhivn me aaven nity hi ras bihari
ras rachaven radhe ke sang gal gal baiyan dari
radha ramn ramn reti banshi vat ki chhavi nyari
kunj kunj me sant viraje hoye radhe dhun pyari
yamuna me snan karun aur yam ki tras mitaun

Vinod Kumar

brij ki un paavan galiyon me radhe radhe gaun,
main radhe radhe gaun main shyama shyama gaun,

dal dal aur pat pat sri radha nam pukare
kaaliyaa mardan rang nath prabhu lila ne bhav taare
surdas hari das bhakt mira ke baje iktare
jo darshan ik bar kare vo apne bhagya sanvare
gopeshvar pagparas bhagvati main gopi ban jaun
brij ki un paavan galiyon me radhe radhe gaun,
main radhe radhe gaun main shyama shyama gaun,

bolo radhe radhe bolo radhe,   radhe radhe bolo radhe
bolo shyama shyama bolo shyama,
shyama shyama bolo shyama

MERA MAN PANCHHI YE CHAHE

dha	ge	n	ti	n	ke	dhi	n	dha	ge	n	ti	n	ke	dhi	n
1	2	3	4	5	6	7	8	1	2	3	4	5	6	7	8
S'	-	-	-	-	N	-	D	D̲	-	N	-	-	-	-	G
he	-	-	-	-	he	-	he	he	-	he	-	-	-	-	hun
M	-	-	D	P	D	M	P	G	-	-	-	-	-	-	-
hun	-	-	hun	hun	-	hun	-	hun	-	-	-	-	-	-	-
G	-	G	-	D	-	D	-	S'	-	S'	-	D	-	D	-
me	-	ra	-	m	n	pn	-	chhi	-	ye	-	cha	-	he	-
S'	-	S'	-	D	-	G	-	P	-	P	-	M	-	-	-
u	d	vrn	-	da	-	v	n	ja	-	un	-	-	-	-	-
P	P	P	-	M	M	M	-	R	-	R	R	S	-	.N	-
bri	j	ki	-	u	n	pa	-	v	n	g	li	yo	-	me	-
.N	-	R	-	P	-	M	-	G	-	G	-	-	-	S'	-
ra	-	dhe	-	ra	-	dhe	-	ga	-	un	-	-	-	main	-
D	-	D	-	S'	-	S'	-	N	-	N	-	-	-	N	-
ra	-	dhe	-	ra	-	dhe	-	ga	-	un	-	-	-	main	-

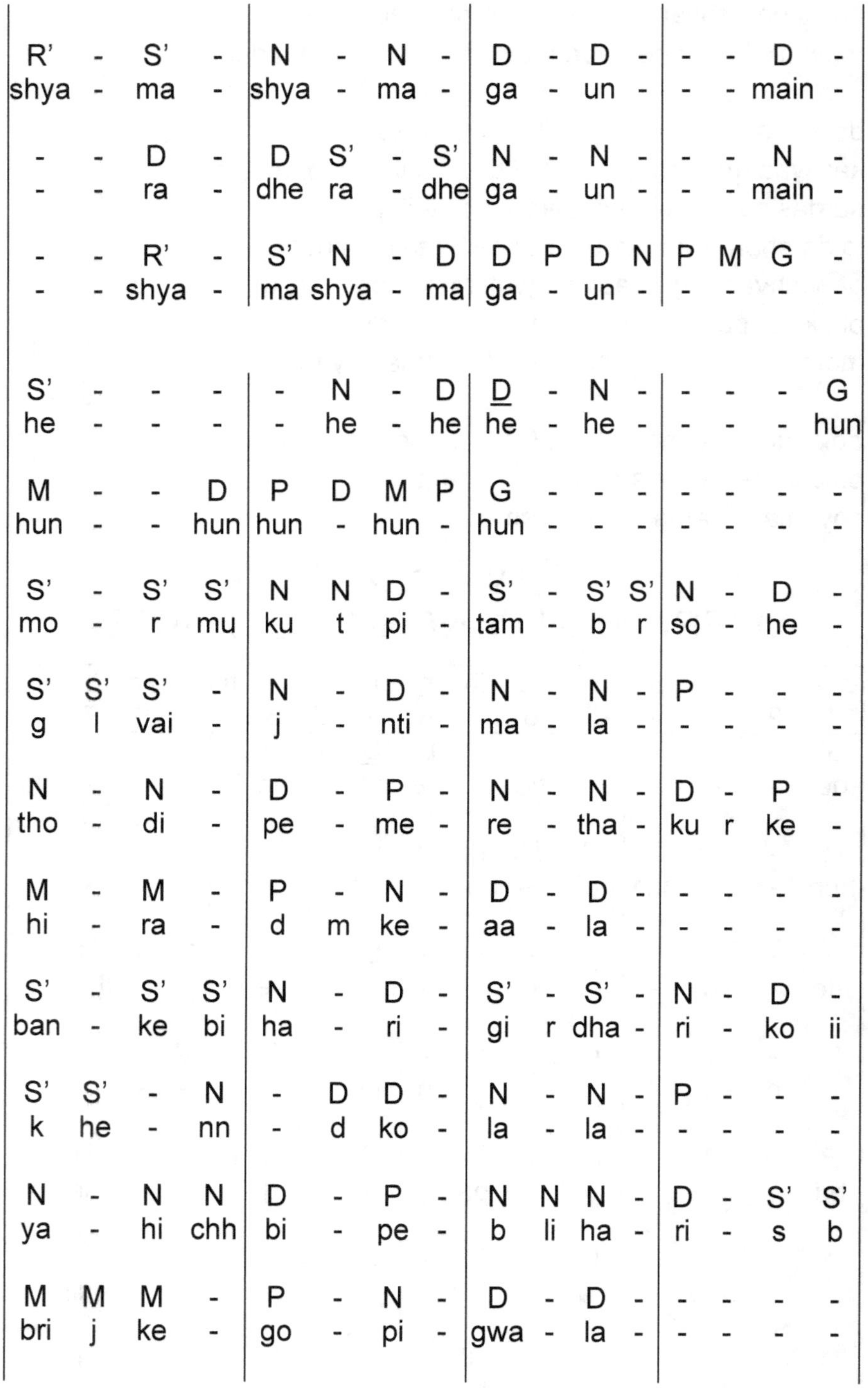

R'	-	S'	-	N	-	N	-	D	-	D	-	-	-	D	-
shya	-	ma	-	shya	-	ma	-	ga	-	un	-	-	-	main	-
-	-	D	-	D	S'	-	S'	N	-	N	-	-	-	N	-
-	-	ra	-	dhe	ra	-	dhe	ga	-	un	-	-	-	main	-
-	-	R'	-	S'	N	-	D	D	P	D	N	P	M	G	-
-	-	shya	-	ma	shya	-	ma	ga	-	un	-	-	-	-	-
S'	-	-	-	-	N	-	D	D̲	-	N	-	-	-	-	G
he	-	-	-	-	he	-	he	he	-	he	-	-	-	-	hun
M	-	-	D	P	D	M	P	G	-	-	-	-	-	-	-
hun	-	-	hun	hun	-	hun	-	hun	-	-	-	-	-	-	-
S'	-	S'	S'	N	N	D	-	S'	-	S'	S'	N	-	D	-
mo	-	r	mu	ku	t	pi	-	tam	-	b	r	so	-	he	-
S'	S'	S'	-	N	-	D	-	N	-	N	-	P	-	-	-
g	l	vai	-	j	-	nti	-	ma	-	la	-	-	-	-	-
N	-	N	-	D	-	P	-	N	-	N	-	D	-	P	-
tho	-	di	-	pe	-	me	-	re	-	tha	-	ku	r	ke	-
M	-	M	-	P	-	N	-	D	-	D	-	-	-	-	-
hi	-	ra	-	d	m	ke	-	aa	-	la	-	-	-	-	-
S'	-	S'	S'	N	-	D	-	S'	-	S'	-	N	-	D	-
ban	-	ke	bi	ha	-	ri	-	gi	r	dha	-	ri	-	ko	ii
S'	S'	-	N	-	D	D	-	N	-	N	-	P	-	-	-
k	he	-	nn	-	d	ko	-	la	-	la	-	-	-	-	-
N	-	N	N	D	-	P	-	N	N	N	-	D	-	S'	S'
ya	-	hi	chh	bi	-	pe	-	b	li	ha	-	ri	-	s	b
M	M	M	-	P	-	N	-	D	-	D	-	-	-	-	-
bri	j	ke	-	go	-	pi	-	gwa	-	la	-	-	-	-	-

Vinod Kumar

G	G	G	G	D	D	D	D	S'	S'	S'	S'	D	D	-	-
yu	g	l	ch	r	n	chh	bi	ni	r	khi	ni	r	khi	-	-
S'	-	-	R'	N	-	-	S'	D	-	-	N	M	P	G	-
o	-	-	-	-	-	-	-	-	-	-	-	-	-	-	-
G	G	G	G	D	D	D	D	S'	S'	S'	S'	D	D	D	D
yu	g	l	ch	r	n	chh	bi	ni	r	khi	ni	r	khi	ni	j
S'	-	S'	S'	D	D	D	G	G	-	P	M	-	-	-	-
ji	-	v	n	s	f	l	b	na	-	un	-	-	-	-	-
P	P	P	-	M	M	M	-	R	-	R	R	S	-	.N	-
bri	j	ki	-	u	n	pa	-	v	n	g	li	yo	-	me	-
.N	-	R	-	P	-	M	-	G	-	G	-	-	-	N	-
ra	-	dhe	-	ra	-	dhe	-	ga	-	un	-	-	-	main	-
D	-	D	-	S'	-	S'	-	N	-	N	-	-	-	N	-
ra	-	dhe	-	ra	-	dhe	-	ga	-	un	-	-	-	main	-
R'	-	S'	-	N	-	N	-	D	-	D	-	-	-	S'	-
shya	-	ma	-	shya	-	ma	-	ga	-	un	-	-	-	main	-
-	-	D	-	D	S'	-	S'	N	-	N	-	-	-	N	-
-	-	ra	-	dhe	ra	-	dhe	ga	-	un	-	-	-	main	-
-	-	R'	-	S'	N	-	D	D	P	D	N	P	M	G	-
-	-	shya	-	ma	shya	-	ma	ga	-	un	-	-	-	-	-
G	-	G	-	D	-	D	-	S'	-	S'	-	D	-	D	-
me	-	ra	-	m	n	pn	-	chhi	-	ye	-	cha	-	he	-
S'	-	S'	-	D	-	G	-	P	-	P	-	M	-	-	-
u	d	vrn	-	da	-	v	n	ja	-	un	-	-	-	-	-
P	P	P	-	-	-	M	-	R	-	R	R	S	-	.N	-
bri	j	ki	-	-	-	pa	-	v	n	g	li	yo	-	me	-
.N	-	R	-	P	-	M	-	G	-	G	-	-	-		
ra	-	dhe	-	ra	-	dhe	-	ga	-	un	-	-	-		

S'	-	-	-	-	N	-	D	D̲	-	N	-	-	-	-	G
he	-	-	-	-	he	-	he	he	-	he	-	-	-	-	hun
M	-	-	D	P	D	M	P	G	-	-	-	-	-	-	-
hun	-	-	hun	hun	-	hun	-	hun	-	-	-	-	-	-	-
S'	-	S'	N	-	N	D	D	S'	S'	S'	-	N	-	D	-
se	-	va	kun	-	j	ni	dhi	b	n	me	-	aa	-	ven	-
S'	-	S'	S'	N	-	D	D	N	-	N	-	P	-	-	-
ni	-	ty	hi	ra	-	s	bi	ha	-	ri	-	-	-	-	-
N	-	N	N	D	-	P	-	N	-	N	-	D	-	P	P
ra	-	s	r	cha	-	ven	-	ra	-	dhe	-	ke	-	sn	g
M	M	M	M	P	-	N	-	D	-	D	-	-	-	-	-
g	l	g	l	bain	-	ya	-	da	-	ri	-	-	-	-	-
S'	-	S'	N	D	D	-	D	S'	-	S'	-	N	-	D	-
ra	-	dha	r	m	n	-	r	m	n	re	-	ti	-	vn	-
S'	-	S'	N	N	-	D	D	N	-	N	-	P	-	-	-
shi	-	v	t	ki	-	chh	bi	nya	-	ri	-	-	-	-	-
N	-	N	D	-	D	P	-	N	-	N	D	S'	-	S'	-
ku	-	nj	ku	-	nj	me	-	sn	-	t	bi	ra	-	je	-
M	M	M	-	P	-	N	N	D	-	D	-	-	-	-	-
ho	ye	ra	-	dhe	-	dhu	ni	pya	-	ri	-	-	-	-	-
G	G	G	-	D	-	D	D	S'	-	S'	S'	D	-	-	-
y	mu	na	-	me	-	i	s	na	-	n	k	run	-	-	-
S'	-	-	R'	N	-	-	S'	D	-	-	N	M	P	G	-
o	-	-	-	-	-	-	-	-	-	-	-	-	-	-	-
G	G	G	-	D	-	D	D	S'	-	S'	S'	D	-	D	D
y	mu	na	-	me	-	i	s	na	-	n	k	run	-	au	r
S'	S'	S'	-	D	-	D	G	G	-	P	M	-	-	-	-
y	m	ki	-	tra	-	s	mi	ta	-	un	-	-	-	-	-

Vinod Kumar

P	P	P	-	M	M	M	-	R	-	R	R	S	-	.N	-
bri	j	ki	-	u	n	pa	-	v	n	g	li	yo	-	me	-

.N	-	R	-	P	-	M	-	G	-	G	-	-	-	N	-
ra	-	dhe	-	ra	-	dhe	-	ga	-	un	-	-	-	main	-

D	-	D	-	S'	-	S'	-	N	-	N	-	-	-	N	-
ra	-	dhe	-	ra	-	dhe	-	ga	-	un	-	-	-	main	-

R'	-	S'	-	N	-	N	-	D	-	D	-	-	-	D	-
shya	-	ma	-	shya	-	ma	-	ga	-	un	-	-	-	main	-

-	-	D	-	D	S'	-	S'	N	-	N	-	-	-	N	-
-	-	ra	-	dhe	ra	-	dhe	ga	-	un	-	-	-	main	-

-	-	R'	-	S'	N	-	D	D	P	D	N	P	M	G	-
-	-	shya	-	ma	shya	-	ma	ga	-	un	-	-	-	-	-

G	-	G	-	D	-	D	-	S'	-	S'	-	D	-	D	-
me	-	ra	-	m	n	pn	-	chhi	-	ye	-	cha	-	he	-

S'	-	S'	-	D	-	G	-	P	-	P	-	M	-	-	-
u	d	vrn	-	da	-	v	n	ja	-	un	-	-	-	-	-

P	P	P	-	M	M	M	-	R	-	R	R	S	-	.N	-
bri	j	ki	-	u	n	pa	-	v	n	g	li	yo	-	me	-

.N	-	R	-	P	-	M	-	G	-	G	-	-	-		
ra	-	dhe	-	ra	-	dhe	-	ga	-	un	-	-	-		

														M	G
														bo	lo

M	-	M	M	-	M	M	G	P	-	P	-	-	-	-	-
ra	-	dhe	ra	-	dhe	bo	lo	ra	-	dhe	-	-	-	-	-

N	-	N	N	-	N	D	P	D	-	D	-	-	-	M	G
ra	-	dhe	ra	-	dhe	bo	lo	ra	-	dhe	-	-	-	bo	lo

M	-	M	M	-	M	M	G	P	-	P	-	-	-	-	-
shya	-	ma	shya	-	ma	bo	lo	shya	-	ma	-	-	-	-	-

N	-	N	N	-	N	D	P	D	-	D	-	-	-
shya	-	ma	shya	-	ma	bo	lo	shya	-	ma	-	-	-

play rest of the song as above.

26. NIJ DHARM PAR CHALNA BATATI

Bhajan
Lyrics: Goswami Bindu Ji
Maharaj
Taal: Rupak
https://youtu.be/UH8AtaYPXM0

Music: Vinod Kumar
Singer: Abhishek Bhama &
Relative
Chord: MDS'   S=C

hame nij dharm par chalna batati roz ramayn
sadaa shubh aachran karna sikhati roz ramayan

jinhe sansar saagar se utar kar paar jana hai
unhe sukh se kinare par lagati roz ramayan

kahin chhavi vishnu ki banki kahin shankar ki hai jhanki
hriday aanand jhule par jhulati roz ramayan

saral kavita ke kunjo me banaa mndir hai hindi ka
jahaan prabhu prem ka darshan karaati roz ramayan

kabhi vedon ke saagar me kabhi gita ki ganga me
kabhi ras 'bindu' me man ko duboti roz ramayan

Vinod Kumar

NIJ DHARM PAR CHALNA BATATI

ti	ti	na	dhin	na	dhin	na	ti	ti	na	dhin	na	dhin	na
1	2	3	4	5	6	7	1	2	3	4	5	6	7
									M	M	-	P	P
									h	me	-	ni	j
N	-	N	N	-	N	-	D	-	D	P	-	M	-
dh	r	m	p	r	ch	l	na	-	b	ta	-	ti	-
G	-	M	D	-	P	-	M	-	M	M	-	P	P
ro	-	z	ra	-	ma	-	y	n	s	da	-	shu	bh
N	-	N	N	-	N	-	D	-	D	P	-	M	-
aa	-	ch	r	n	k	r	na	-	si	kha	-	ti	-
G	-	M	D	-	P	-	M	-					
ro	-	z	ra	-	ma	-	y	n					
interlude::									-	M	-	P	-
D	N	D	P	-	M	-	G	-	G	M	-	P	-
D	N	D	P	-	M	-	M	-	-	M	-	P	-
D	N	D	P	-	M	-	G	-	G	M	-	P	
D	N	D	P	-	M	-	M	-					
									D	D	-	N	-
									jin	hen	-	sn	-
S'	-	S'	S'	-	S'	-	S'	-	S'	S'	-	S'	-
sa	-	r	sa	-	g	r	se	-	u	t	r	k	r
R'	-	R'	S'	-	N	-	D	-	M	M	-	P	P
pa	-	r	ja	-	na	-	hai	-	u	nhe	-	su	kh
N	-	N	N	-	N	-	D	-	D	P	-	M	-
se	-	ki	na	-	re	-	p	r	l	ga	-	ti	-
G	-	M	D	-	P	-	M	-	M	M	-	P	P
ro	-	z	ra	-	ma	-	y	n	h	me	-	ni	j
N	-	N	N	-	N	-	D	-	D	P	-	M	-
dh	r	m	p	r	ch	l	na	-	b	ta	-	ti	-

G	-	M	D	-	P	-	M	-	M	M	-	P	P
ro	-	z	ra	-	ma	-	y	n	s	da	-	shu	bh

N	-	N	N	-	N	-	D	-	D	P	-	M	-
aa	-	ch	r	n	k	r	na	-	si	kha	-	ti	-

G	-	M	D	-	P	-	M	-
ro	-	z	ra	-	ma	-	y	n

interlude: as above.

D	D	-	N	N
k	hin	-	chh	vi

S'	-	S'	S'	-	S'	-	S'	-	S'	S'	-	S'	-
vi	-	shnu	ki	-	ban	-	ki	-	k	hin	-	shn	-

R'	-	R'	S'	-	N	-	D	-	M	M	-	P	-
k	r	ki	hai	-	jhan	-	ki	-	hr	d	y	aa	-

N	-	N	N	-	N	-	D	-	D	P	-	M	-
nn	-	d	jhu	-	le	-	p	r	jhu	la	-	ti	-

G	-	M	D	-	P	-	M	-	M	M	-	P	P
ro	-	z	ra	-	ma	-	y	n	h	me	-	ni	j

N	-	N	N	-	-	-
dh	r	m	p	r	-	-

interlude: as above.

D	D	-	N	N
s	r	l	k	vi

S'	-	S'	S'	-	S'	-	S'	-	S'	S'	-	S'	-
ta	-	ke	kun	-	jo	-	me	-	b	na	-	mn	-

R'	-	R'	S'	-	N	-	D	-	M	M	-	P	P
di	r	hai	hin	-	di	-	ka	-	j	ha	-	pr	bhu

N	-	N	N	-	N	-	D	-	D	P	-	M	-
pre	-	m	ka	-	d	r	sh	n	k	ra	-	ti	-

G	-	M	D	-	P	-	M	-	M	M	-	P	P
ro	-	z	ra	-	ma	-	y	n	h	me	-	ni	j

Vinod Kumar

1	2	3	4	5	6	7	8	9	10	11	12	13	14
N̲	-	N̲	N̲	-	-	-							
dh	r	m	p	r	-	-							

interlude: as above.

1	2	3	4	5	6	7	8	9	10	11	12	13	14
									D	D	-	N̲	-
									k	bhi	-	ve	-
S'	-	S'	S'	-	S'	-	S'	-	S'	S'	-	S'	-
don	-	ke	sa	-	g	r	me	-	k	bhi	-	gi	-
R'	-	R'	S'	-	N̲	-	D	-	M	M	-	P	P
ta	-	ki	gn	-	ga	-	me	-	k	bhi	-	r	s
N̲	-	N̲	N̲	-	N̲	-	D	-	D	P	-	M	-
bin	-	du	me	-	m	n	ko	-	du	bo	-	ti	-
G̲	-	M	D	-	P	-	M	-	M	M	-	P	P
ro	-	z	ra	-	ma	-	y	n	h	me	-	ni	j
N̲	-	N̲	N̲	-	-	-							
dh	r	m	p	r	-	-							

27. NIRBAL KE PRAN PUKAR RAHE

Hari Bhajan   Singer: Gautam
Taal: Kaharwa   Chord: P<u>N</u>R'   S=C#
https://youtu.be/2ZXB6IKP8MQ

aesi bhakti de do mujhe shyam ke japta rahun main tera naam

safal ho meri bhakti bulale mujhko gokul dhaam

nirbal ke pran pukar rahe, jagdish hare jagdish hare

aakash himaly sagar me, prithvi pataal charaachar me

ye bol madhur gunjaar rahe -2, jagdish hare jagdish hare

jab door drishti ho jati hai, jalti kheti hariyati hai

tute na lagaa ye taar rahe -2, jagdish hare jagdish hare

ho, mujhme tujhme antar ye hai main nar hun tum narayan ho

main hun us jag ke hathon me, jiska tu uddhar kare

jagdish hare jagdish hare jagdish hare jagdish hare

NIRBAL KE PRAN PUKAR RAHE

dha	ge	n	ti	n	ke	dhi	n	dha	ge	n	ti	n	ke	dhi	n
1	2	3	4	5	6	7	8	1	2	3	4	5	6	7	8

R'R'   G'S'<u>N</u> R'S'<u>G</u>' R'   S'<u>N</u>   PM
aesi   bhakti de---   do mujhe shyam

M MMM MP <u>N</u>   <u>D</u>P P
ke japta rahun main tera naam

Vinod Kumar

MG̲M   P MPG̲ G̲MP MMM S'S'S' S'R'G̲' R'S'
safal   ho meri bhakti bulale mujhko gokul dhaam

G̲'R'S'D PS'N̲   N̲
mujhko gokul dhaam

N̲S'S' R' S'N̲ N̲NS'N̲ DP
nirbal ke pran pukar rahe

N̲S'S' R'G̲'M'R' S'N̲   N̲NS'N̲   DP
nirbal ke----   pran puka---r rahe

PPMG̲-P PP PPD-P   MM MMMG̲-PP PP PPDS'S' N̲N̲
jagdish   hare jagdish   hare jagdi--sh   hare jagdish   hare

 R'R'G̲'   M'G̲'R'   R'G̲'M' R'S'
aakash   himalay   sagar   me

R' R'G̲'   M'G̲'R'   S'N̲S'S' S'
aakash   himalay   sagar   me

S'S'S'   S'DP   PPS'S'N̲   N̲
prithvi pataal charaachar me

D N̲N̲ DN̲   N̲DS'N̲ DP S' S'G̲'R' S'N̲ N̲GPD N̲DP
ye bol madhur gunjaar rahe ye bol   madhur gunjaar rahe

PPMG̲-P PP PPD-P   MM MMMG̲-PP PP PPDS'S' N̲N̲
jagdish   hare jagdish   hare jagdish   hare jagdish   hare

 R' R'R' G̲'M' G̲'R'R'N̲ R' G̲'M'S' S'
o jab   door dri-shti- ho ja-ti   hai

R'R' G̲'M' G̲'R'R'N̲ R'S'N̲ S'S'   S'
jab   door dri-shti- ho-- ja-ti   hai

S'S'S' PP S'<u>N</u>S'<u>N</u> <u>N</u>
jalti   kheti hariyati hai

D<u>N</u> <u>N</u> D<u>N</u> <u>N</u> DS'<u>N</u> DP D<u>N</u>R' S' <u>NN</u> <u>N</u> <u>G</u>PD <u>N</u>DP
tute na lagaa ye taar rahe tute na lagaa ye taar rahe

PPM<u>G</u>-P PP PPD-P   MM   MMM<u>G</u>-PP PP PPDS'S' <u>NN</u>
jagdish   hare jagdish   hare jagdish   hare jagdish   hare

R'   R'R'<u>G</u>'M' <u>G</u>'R'R'   R'<u>G</u>'M' R'S' S'
ho, mujhme   tujhme   antar   ye   hai

R'   R'R'<u>G</u>'M'   <u>G</u>'R'R'   R'<u>N</u>S'S' S'   S'
ho, mujhme   tujhme   antar   ye   hai

S'   S'S' DP   P   S'S'<u>NN</u>   <u>N</u>
main nar hun tum narayan ho

D<u>N</u>   <u>N</u>   D<u>N</u> <u>NN</u> DS' <u>N</u>DPM P
main hun us jag ke hathon me

<u>N</u>S'R'   <u>N</u>   <u>NN</u> <u>NN</u>PM <u>G</u>M P<u>N</u><u>D</u>P   P
main-- hun us jag--- ke- ha-thon- me

MMM   M<u>G</u> PDP   MM
jiska   tu- uddhar kre

PPM<u>G</u>-P PP PPD-P   MM MMM<u>G</u>-PP PP PPDS'S' <u>NN</u>
jagdish   hare jagdish   hare jagdish   hare jagdish   hare

Vinod Kumar

28. O SHANKER MERE KAB HONGE

film: Bairag (1976)
Lyrics: Anand Bakshi
Taal: Kaharwa
https://youtu.be/I16FRbPQ3Ew

Music: Kalyanji Anandji
Singer: Mahendra Kapoor
Chord: SGD GPN S=F#

jeevan path par sham savere chhaye hain ghanghor andhere
o shankar mere kab honge darshan tere

main muradh tu antaryami, main sevak tu mera swami
kahe mujhse nata toda, man chhoda mandir bhi chhoda
kitni door-2 lagaaye tune ja kailash pe dere

tere dware jyot jagaate, yug beete tere gun gaate
na mangun main heere moti, maangun bas thodi si jyoti
khaali haath na jaaunga main-2 data dwar se tere

O SHANKER MERE KAB HONGE

dha	ge	n	ti	n	ke	dhi	n	dha	ge	n	ti	n	ke	dhi	n
1	2	3	4	5	6	7	8	1	2	3	4	5	6	7	8

prelude:
S'---- R' S' G' ----
R' ---- S' ---- N D R'----
S' N D S' ----

S'-S'S' R'S' S'-D DS'G' S'DP GP   D   DGPDM* GRGRS
jeevan path par   sham savere chhaye hain ghanghor andhere

D- P- M* P D P- M*-G M* P-- G R S
aa----------   aa-----------   music

music: GG G –G G R –R R .D –G –R S -2
flute: G M*- M*D- M*D- M*G GM*D- M*G- RG-
GG G –G G R –R R .D –G –R S

GG G G G R R R
D M* G R S

 S SSR   GGRGGD- PDM*G RG   RS   RGRS   SS
o shankar mere------------,---   kab honge darshan   tere

G GG GG GG GR   RGG RSG
jeevan path par sham savere

G GG GG GG GR RGG   PP   P   PPGDP GRGRS
jeevan path par sham savere chhaye hain ghanghor andhere

S SSR   GGRGGD- PDM*G RG   RS   RGRS SS
o shankar mere--------------   kab honge darshan tere
interlude:
GG G G G R R R .D G R S
GG G G G R R R D M* G R G M* D

S'   NDD   D PGGDP   S   SRGG D M*GRG RSS
main murakh tu antaryami, main sevak tu   mera   swami

MM MM M MM*D MGRM MM MM   MMM   M*D MG
kahe mujhse nata   toda,   man chhoda mandir bhi chhoda

S'S'S' S'------NDS'
kitni   door------------

S'S'S' S'   S'S'NR'S' DPP P PPP   D GGD --- M*GR
kitni door lagaaye   tune ja kailash pe dere

S SSR   GGRGGD- PDM*G RG   RS   RGRS SS
o shankar mere   kab honge darshan tere

interlude:
sitar: S R M M M M D M* G – RG- R S
        S R M M M D M* G D M* G R G M* D –

Vinod Kumar

S'N DD D PG   GDP   SS SRG D-M*G RG RSS
tere dware jyot jagaate, yug beete tere   gun gaate

M MM   M   MM*D MGRM MM   M MM M*D MG
na mangun main heere   moti, maangun bas thodi si-   jyoti

S'S' S'S' S' S'R'G'R' S'
khali hath na jaun-ga main

bin: SGG SRR .NSS .NSS x 3
     S'NDPMGRS R-G-M*-D-

S'S'   S'S'   S' S'NR'S'D P   PP   PP   P GGD- M*GRS
khaali haath na jaaunga   main   data dwar se tere------------

S SSR   GGRGGD- PDM*G RG RS   RGRS SS
o shankar mere------------   kab honge darshan tere

music: S R G P D S'- (R'S') x8
        S' N D P G R S M

MM MM MM*DM*M   GM
kab honge darshan   tere

DD DD   DD M*G   M* D
kab honge darshan   tere

S'S' S'S'   S'R'G' R'S'   NS'
kab honge darshan   tere -2

music:
R'S'ND NDPM PMGR GRS.D S---- R ---- S -----

29. PREM MUDIT MAN SE KAHO

Sri Ram Bhajan
Taal: Daadra
https://youtu.be/U1WN4-fSw-4

Singer: Smt MS Subbalakshmi
Chord: RM*D   S= G

prem mudit man se kaho ram ram ram
sri ram ram ram sri ram ram ram
sri ra---m ram ram

paap kate dukh mite le ke ram naam,
bhav samudra sukhad naav ek ram naam
sri ram ram ram sri ram ram ram,
sri ram ram ram sri ra---m ram ram

param shanti sukh nidhan nitya ram naam,
niradhar ko aadhar ek ram naam
sri ram ram ram sri ram ram ram,
sri ram ram ram sri ra---m ram ram

param gupya param iisht mantra ram naam,
sant hridaya sadaa basat ek ram naam
sri ram ram ram sri ram ram ram,
sri ram ram ram sri ra---m ram ram

mahadev satata japat divya ram naam,
kashi marat mukt karat chdhat ram naam
sri ram ram ram sri ram ram ram,
sri ram ram ram sri ra---m ram ram

maat pita bandhu sakhaa sab hi ram naam,
bhakt janan jivan dhan ek ram naam
sri ram ram ram sri ram ram ram,
sri ram ram ram sri ra---m ram ram

Vinod Kumar

PREM MUDIT MAN SE KAHO

dha	dhi	na	dha	tun	na	dha	dhi	na	dha	tun	na
1	2	3	4	5	6	1	2	3	4	5	6

GG GGG RM* G RSR M*M* GRG M*
prem mudit man se kaho ram   ram   ram

M*   M*M* M*GM* DP P DM* RR M*G G RGM*G RSR M*G
sri ram   ram   ram sri ram ram ram   sri ra---m   ram   ram

M*M* DD ND NN D D D<u>R</u>'N   DP
paap kate dukh mite le ke ram   naam,

M*M*   M*M*GM*   DDD M*M* GG RSR M*G
bhav   samudra   sukhad naav ek ram   naam

G GG GRG M* M* M*M* M*GM* M*DP
sri ram ram ram sri   ram   ram   ram,

P DM* RM* M*G G RGM*G RSR M*G
sri ram ram ram sri ra---m   ram   ram

GM*M* DD   DN DNN   DD D<u>R</u>'N   DP
param shanti sukh nidhan nitya ram   naam,

M*M*M*GM* D DM*G GG RSR   M*G
niradhar   ko aadhar ek ram   naam

G GG GRG M* M* M*M* M*GM* M*DP
sri ram ram ram sri ram   ram   ram,

P DM* RM* M*G G RGM*G RSR M*G
sri ram ram ram sri ra---m   ram   ram

GM*M* DD   DND NN DD   D<u>R</u>'N DP
param gupya param iisht mantra ram   naam,

M*M* M*GM* M*D M*M*M* GG RSR M*G
sant hridaya sadaa basat ek ram naam

G GG GRG M* M* M*M* M*GM* M*DP
sri ram ram ram sri ram ram ram,

P DM* RM* M*G G RGM*G RSR M*G
sri ram ram ram sri ra---m ram ram

 GM*DD DND NNN DD D<u>R</u>'N DP
mahadev satata japat divya ram naam,

M*M* M*GM* P-D M*M*G GM*G RSR M*G
kashi marat mukt karat chdhat ram naam

G GG GRG M* M* M*M* M*GM* M*DP
sri ram ram ram sri ram ram ram,

P DM* RM* M*G G RGM*G RSR M*G
sri ram ram ram sri ra---m ram ram

M*M* DD ND NN NN D D <u>R</u>'N DP
maat pita bandhu sakhaa sab hi ram naam

M*M* M*GM* DDM* M*G GG RSR M*G
bhakt janan jivan dhan ek ram naam

G GG GRG M* M* M*M* M*GM* M*DP
sri ram ram ram sri ram ram ram,

P DM* RM* M*G G RGM*G RSR M*G
sri ram ram ram sri ra---m ram ram

Vinod Kumar

30. RE MAN YE DO DIN KA MELA

Bhajan
Lyrics: Rajeshwaranand Swami
Taal: Kaharwa

Music: Rajeshwaranand Swami
Singer: Rajeshwaranand Swami
Chord: RMD G̲P̲N P̲N̲R'
S=C#

https://youtu.be/DFlwwR_ZLZQ

re man ye do din ka mela rahega,
kaayam ye jag ka jhamela rahega

saathi hain mitra ye gang ke jal bindu paan tak
ardhangani badhegi kewal makaan tak
ghar ke sab log chalenge ishmshan tak
beta bhi haq nibhayega to agnidaan tak
isse to aage bhajan hi hai saathi
hari ke bhajan bin akela rahega

RE MAN YE DO DIN KA MELA

dha	ge	n	ti	n	ke	dhi	n	dha	ge	n	ti	n	ke	dhi	n
1	2	3	4	5	6	7	8	1	2	3	4	5	6	7	8

DD   D D<u>N</u>   DD D   D DD P<u>N</u>D DD
saathi hain mitra gang ke   jal bindu paan tak

<u>NNNN</u>   DNN   <u>ND</u>   P<u>N</u>D DD
ardhangani badhegi kewal makaan tak

R'<u>R</u>'R'R'   R'   R'<u>R</u>'   R'R'   R'R'R'   R'R' S'R'<u>G</u>'R' <u>ND</u>
parivar   ke sab   log   chalenge ishm sha--n tak

DD D DD DDDD   D DD<u>N</u> S'-<u>N</u> DD
beta bhi haq nibhayega to agnidaan   tak

<u>N</u>—DPM<u>G</u>R
aa------------

R<u>G</u>M <u>G</u> PP DDD   D D PM<u>N</u>-
isse   to   aage bhajan hi hai saathi

<u>NN</u> D PP   M PD   DDP M<u>G</u>M <u>G</u>R
hari ke bhajan bin---   akela   rahega----

		R	<u>G</u>	M	-	<u>G</u>	P	-	-	-	P	-	P	-
		re	-	mn	-	ye	do	-	-	-	di	n	ka	-
-	-	- D	-	P	-	D	M	-	-	-	P	D	<u>N</u>	-
-	-	- me	-	la	-	r	he	-	-	-	ga	-	-	-
-	-	- <u>N</u>	-	D	-	P	M	-	M	-	D	-	-	-
-	-	- ka	-	yam	-	ye	j	-	g	-	ka	-	-	-
-	-	D <u>N</u>	-	D	-	P	<u>G</u>	-	M	-	<u>G</u>	-	R	-
-	-	jh me	-	la	-	r	he	-	ga	-	-	-	-	-
-	-													
-	-													

interlude: <u>N</u>—PD—MP—<u>G</u>M-R   <u>N</u>—PD—MP—

Vinod Kumar

1	2	3	4	5	6	7	8	9	10	11	12	13	14	15	16
														D	-
														sa	-
D	-	D	-	-	S'	-	N	D	-	-	D	P	-	M	M
thi	-	hai	-	-	mi	-	tr	gn	-	-	g	ke	-	j	l
D	-	D	-	-	S'	-	N	D	D	-	-	-	-	M	M
bin	-	du	-	-	pa	-	n	t	k	-	-	-	-	a	r
D	-	-	-	D	S'	-	N	D	-	D	-	-	-	M	-
dhan	-	-	-	g	ni	-	b	dhe	-	gi	-	-	-	ke	-
D	D	-	-	D	S'	-	N	D	D	-	-	-	-	D	N
v	l	-	-	m	ka	-	n	t	k	-	-	-	-	p	ri
S'	-	-	S'	S'	-	S'	N	S'	-	S'	S'	S'	-	N	D
va	-	-	r	ke	-	s	b	lo	-	g	ch	le	-	ge	-
-	-	D	-	N	S'	-	N	D	D	-	-	-	-	R'	-
-	-	i	sh	m	sha	-	n	t	k	-	-	-	-	be	-
R'	-	R'	-	-	N	N	D	P	-	-	M	P	D	D	-
ta	-	bhi	-	-	h	k	ni	bha	-	-	ye	ga	-	to	-
-	-	P	P	P	M	-	G	R	R	-	-	-	-	-	-
-	-	a	g	ni	da	-	n	t	k	-	-	-	-	-	-
-	-	-	R	G	M	-	G	P	-	-	-	P	-	-	-
-	-	-	i	s	se	-	to	aa	-	-	-	ge	-	j	-
-	-	D	D	D	P	-	D	M	-	-	-	P	D	N	
-	-	bh	j	n	hi	-	hai	sa	-	-	-	thi	-	-	
-	-	-	N	N	D	-	P	M	-	-	-	D	-	-	-
-	-	-	h	ri	ke	-	bh	jn	-	-	-	bin	-	-	-
-	-	D	N	-	D	-	P	G	-	M	-	G	-	R	-
-	-	a	ke	-	la	-	r	he	-	ga	-	-	-	-	-
-	-														
-	-														

31. SHYAM MANOHAR SE MAN KO

Krishna Bhajan
Lyrics: Goswami Bindu Ji
Taal: Daadra
https://youtu.be/CggMGLadt6c

Music: Vinod Kumar Bhama
Singer: Abhishek Bhama
Chord: SM <u>GPN</u>   S=C#

shyam manohar se man ko lagaaya nahin
to maza tune nar tan ka paaya nahin

suyash unka shravan me samaaya nahin
kirti gungaan unka to gaaya nahin
dhyan me inke yadi tu lubhaaya nahin
unke charno ki seva me aaya nahin
to maza tune nar tan ka paaya nahin

unke archan ka anuraag chaaya nahin
dwar par unke sar ko jhukaya nahin
daas ya mitr unka kahaaya nahin
unpe sarvaswa apna lutaaya nahin
to maza tune nar tan ka paaya nahin

prem me unke jeevan bitaaya nahin
vednaamay hriday ko banaaya nahin
ashru ka 'bindu' drig se giraaya nahin
unki virhagni me tan jalaaya nahin
to maza tune nar tan ka paaya nahin

Vinod Kumar

SHYAM MANOHAR SE MAN KO

dha	dhi	na	dha	tun	na	dha	dhi	na	dha	tun	na
1	2	3	4	5	6	1	2	3	4	5	6
									M	-	S
									shya	-m	m
S	M	M	-	M	-	M	P	M	G	-	G
no	-	h	r	se	-	m	n	ko	-	-	l
G	M	P	-	-	M	P	-	-	S'	-	S'
ga	-	ya	-	-	n	hin	-	-	to	-	m
S'	N	N	P	P	-	M	G	M	P	P	-
za	-	tu	-	ne	-	n	r	t	n	ka	-
M	-	M	-	-	M	M	-	-			
pa	-	ya	-	-	n	hin	-	-			

interlude: S'S' NS'NP-P- M- GMP- M-M-M-M- -2

dha	dhi	na	dha	tun	na	dha	dhi	na	dha	tun	na
1	2	3	4	5	6	1	2	3	4	5	6
											N
											su
N	N	N	-	N	-	D	D	-	P	-	M
y	sh	u	n	ka	-	shr	v	n	me	-	s
G	M	P	-	-	M	M	-	-	N	-	N
ma	-	ya	-	-	n	hin	-	-	ki	-	rti
N	-	N	-	-	N	D	-	P	-	-	M
gu	n	ga	-	-	n	u	n	ka	-	-	jo
G	M	P	-	-	M	M	-	-	N	-	N
ga	-	ya	-	-	n	hin	-	-	dhya	-	n
N	-	N	-	N	-	D	D	P	-	-	M
me	-	i	n	ke	-	y	di	tu	-	-	lu
G	M	P	-	-	M	M	-	-	S'	-	S'
bha	-	ya	-	-	n	hin	-	-	u	n	ke
S'	-	S'	-	-	S'	N	S'	N	P	-	P
ch	r	no	-	-	ki	se	-	va	-	-	me

P	N	S'	-	-	N	S'	-	-	S'	-	S'
aa	-	ya	-	-	n	hin	-	-	to	-	m
S'	N	N	P	P	-	M	G	M	P	P	-
za	-	tu	-	ne	-	n	r	t	n	ka	-
M	-	M	-	-	M	M	-	-	M	-	S
pa	-	ya	-	-	n	hin	-	-	shya	-m	m
S	M	M	-	M	-	M	P	M	G	-	G
nau	-	h	r	se	-	m	n	ko	-	-	l
G	M	P	-	-	M	P	-	-	S'	-	S'
ga	-	ya	-	-	n	hin	-	-	to	-	m
S'	N	N	P	P	-	M	G	M	P	P	-
za	-	tu	-	ne	-	n	r	t	n	ka	-
M	-	M	-	-	M	M	-	-			
pa	-	ya	-	-	n	hin	-	-			

interlude: S'S' NS'NP-P- M- GMP- M-M-M-M- -2

									N	-	N
									u	n	ke
N	-	N	-	N	-	D	D	P	-	-	M
a	r	ch	n	ka	-	a	nu	ra	-	-	g
G	M	P	-	-	M	M	-	-	N	-	N
chha	-	ya	-	-	n	hin	-	-	dwa	-	r
N	-	N	-	N	-	D	-	P	-	-	M
p	r	u	n	ke	-	s	r	ko	-	-	jhu
G	M	P	-	-	M	M	-	-	N	-	N
ka	-	ya	-	-	n	hin	-	-	da	-	s
N	-	N	-	-	N	D	-	P	-	-	M
ya	-	mi	-	-	tr	u	n	ka	-	-	k

Vinod Kumar

G	M	P	-	-	M	M	-	-	S'	-	S'
ha	-	ya	-	-	n	hin	-	-	u	n	pe
S'	-	S'	-	-	S'	N	S'	N	P	-	P
s	r	v	-	-	sw	a	p	na	-	-	lu
P	N	S'	-	-	N	S'	-	-	S'	-	S'
ta	-	ya	-	-	n	hin	-	-	to	-	m
S'	N	N	P	P	-	M	G	M	P	P	-
za	-	tu	-	ne	-	n	r	t	n	ka	-
M	-	M	-	-	M	M	-	-	M	-	S
pa	-	ya	-	-	n	hin	-	-	shya	-m	m
S	M	M	-	M	-	M	P	M	G	-	
nau	-	h	r	se	-	m	n	ko	-	-	

interlude: S'S' NS'NP-P- M- GMP- M-M-M-M- -2

									N	-	N
									pre	-	m
N	-	N	-	N	-	D	-	P	-	-	M
me	-	u	n	ke	-	Ji	-	v	n	-	bi
G	M	P	-	-	M	M	-	-	N	-	N
ta	-	ya	-	-	n	hin	-	-	ve	-	d
N	-	N	-	-	N	D	-	P	-	-	M
na	-	m	y	-	hr	d	y	ko	-	-	b
G	M	P	-	-	M	M	-	-	N	-	N
na	-	ya	-	-	n	hin	-	-	a	-	shru
N	-	N	-	-	N	D	D	P	-	-	M
ka	-	bin	-	-	du	dri	g	se	-	-	gi
G	M	P	-	-	M	M	-	-	S'	-	S'
ra	-	ya	-	-	n	hin	-	-	u	n	ki
S'	-	S'	-	-	S'	N	S'	N	P	-	P
vi	r	ha	-	-	gni	me	-	t	n	-	j

P	N	S'	-	-	N	S'	-	-	S'	-	S'
la	-	ya	-	-	n	hin	-	-	to	-	m
S'	N	N	P	P	-	M	G	M	P	P	-
za	-	tu	-	ne	-	n	r	t	n	ka	-
M	-	M	-	-	M	M	-	-	M	-	S
pa	-	ya	-	-	n	hin	-	-	shya	-m	m
S	M	M	-	M	-	M	P	M	G	-	
no	-	h	r	se	-	m	n	ko	-	-	

Vinod Kumar

32. TERI MURALI DI MITTHI TAAN

Krishna Bhajan   Chord: M<u>D</u>S' <u>GPN</u>   S=C#
Taal: Kaharwa
https://youtu.be/ECFit5FEZ8w

teri murali di -2 mithi mithi taan te taan te
main taan ho ho gayi qurbaan ve,
main taan ho gayi ho gayi ho gayi qurbaan ve

murali vajaa ke haay dil sada lai gaya
aankh de ishaare naal sab kuj kah gaya
hun jieeniyaan (living) main lai lai tera naam ve naam ve
main taan ho ho gayi qurbaan ve,

chhaddin na umar bhar kadi mera saath ve
aave na vichhode vaali kadi shyama raat ve
tere kadmaan ch meri jind jaan ve
main taan ho ho gayi qurbaan ve,

kar gaye ghaayal naina vaale teer ve
pyaar tera paake meri khuli taqdir ve
hove kadnaan ch zindagi di shaam ve
main taan ho ho gayi qurbaan ve,

TERI MURALI DI MITTHI TAAN

dhage	nti	nke	dhin	dhage	nti	nke	dhin	dhage	nti	nke	dhin	dhage	nti	nke	dhin
12	34	56	78	12	34	56	78	12	34	56	78	12	34	56	78

prelude: <u>DD</u> PM <u>DD</u> PM <u>DD</u> PM P--,   <u>DD</u> PM <u>DD</u> PM <u>DD</u> PM M---

				M		M		M	-S'	-	S'	-	-	M	M
				te		ri		mur	-li	-	di	-	-	te	ri
M	-S'	-	S'	S'	S'	<u>N</u>	D	<u>N</u>	-	-	<u>D</u>	P	M	-	-
mur	-li	-	di	mi	thi	mi	thi	ta	-	-	n	te	-	-	-
<u>N</u>	-	-	<u>D</u>	P	M	<u>G</u>	G	M	-	P	-	<u>D</u>	-	P	M
ta	-	-	n	te	-	main	ta	ho	-	ho	-	g	ii	qu	r
P	M	-	M	M	P	<u>G</u>	G	M	M	P	P	<u>D</u>	<u>D</u>	P	M
ba	-	-	n	ve	-	main	ta	ho	gaii	ho	gaii	ho	gaii	qu	r
P	M	-	M	M	-										
ba	-	-	n	ve	-										

interlude: <u>DD</u> PM <u>DD</u> PM <u>DD</u> PM P---

    <u>DD</u> PM <u>DD</u> PM <u>DD</u> PM M- <u>D</u>- S'-

				S'M'	M'	M'		<u>G'</u>	G'	R'	<u>N</u>	R'	R'	M'	M'	<u>R'</u>	-S'	S'	-
				mur	li	v		ja	ke	ha	y	di	l	sa	da	lai	-g	or	-
-	<u>DD</u>	<u>D</u>	<u>D</u>	<u>N</u>	<u>N</u>	P	M	-	<u>GM</u>	-P	-P	M	-M	M	-				
-	ankh	de	i	sha	re	na	l	-	sb	-ku	-j	kh	-g	or	-				
-	-	M	M	-	MS'	S'	S'	S'	S'	<u>N</u>	D	<u>N</u>	-	-	<u>D</u>				
-	-	hu	n	-	jini	yan	main	lai	lai	te	ra	na	-	-	m				
P	M	-	-	<u>N</u>	-	-	<u>D</u>	P	M	<u>G</u>	G	M	-	P	-				
ve	-	-	-	na	-	-	m	ve	-	maintam		ho	-	ho	-				
<u>D</u>	-	P	M	P	M	-	M	M	P	<u>G</u>	G	M	M	P	P				
ga	ii	qu	r	ba	-	-	n	ve	-	maintam		ho	gaii	ho	gaii				
<u>D</u>	<u>D</u>	P	M	P	M	-	M	M	-										
ho	gaii	qu	r	ba	-	-	n	ve	-										
		S'	M'M'	M'	<u>G'</u>	G'	R'	<u>N</u>	-	R'R'	M'	M'	<u>R'</u>	-S'	S'	-			
		chh	ddi,na	u	m	r	bh	r	-	kdi	-me	-ra	sa	-th	ve	-			

Vinod Kumar

-	D	DD	D	N	N	P	M	-	GM	-P	-P	M	-M	M	-
-	aa	ve,na	-vi	chho	de	va	li	-	kdi	shya	ma	ra	-t	ve	-

-	-	M	M	-	MS'	S'	S'	S'	S'	N	D	N	-	-	D
-	-	te	re	-	qd	maan	ch	me	ri	jin	d	ja	-	-	n

P	M	-	-	N	-	-	D	P	M	G	G	M	-	P	-
ve	-	-	-	ja	-	-	n	ve	-	main	ta	ho	-	ho	-

D	-	P	M	P	M	-	M	M	P	G	G	M	M	P	P
ga	ii	qu	r	ba	-	-	n	ve	-	main	ta	ho gaii		ho gaii	

D	D	P	M	P	M	-	M	M	-						
ho	gaii	qu	r	ba	-	-	n	ve	-						

	S'M'	M'	M'	G'	-	R'	N	-	R'	R'M'	M'	R'	-S'	S'	-
	kr	g	ye	gha	-	y	l	-	nai	nan,va	-le	ti	-r	ve	-

-	D	DD	D	N	N	P	M	-	GM	-P	-P	M	-M	M	-
-	pya	r,te	ra	pa	ke	me	ri	-	khulli	-t	q	di	-r	ve	-

-	-	M	M	-	MS'	S'	S'	S'	S'	N	D	N	-	-	D
-	-	ho	ve	-	qd	maan	ch	zin	d	gi	di	sha	-	-	m

P	M	-	-	N	-	-	D	P	M	G	G	M	-	P	-
ve	-	-	-	sha	-	-	m	ve	-	main	ta	ho	-	ho	-

D	-	P	M	P	M	-	M	M	P	G	G	M	M	P	P
ga	ii	qu	r	ba	-	-	n	ve	-	main	ta	ho gaii		ho gaii	

D	D	P	M	P	M	-	M	M	-						
ho	gaii	qu	r	ba	-	-	n	ve	-						

33. UJJAIN KE RAJA BABA

Shiv Bhajan   Chord: MDS'   S=C
Taal: Kaharwa
https://youtu.be/A5MuLGdg73M

akaal mrityu vo mare jo kaam kare chaandal ka
aur kaal uska kya bighade jo bhagat ho mahaakaal ka

ujjain ke raja kabhi kirpa najariya dukhiya pe dalna re -2
raja mahaaraja kabhi kirpa najariya dukhiya pe dalna re

parvati pati shiv ji hain pyare
kailash par mere bhole viraje, mere bhole viraje
mankaameshvar baba man ki muraadein
mahaaleshvar baba man ki muradein jholi me dalna re
ujjain ke raja kabhi kirpa najariya dukhiya pe dalna re

naino me jwala aankhon me jwala
jata me ganga pahne mrigchhala bhole pahne mrigchhala
khulti hai jab unki tisri vo ankhiyan-2 tandav kar dalna re
ujjain ke raja kabhi kirpa najariya dukhiya pe dalna re

peete hain pyae bhar bhar ke bhangiya
lagaaye dam bhole din aur ratiyaan, bhole din aur ratiyaan
baba tera bhagat hun main bahut deevana
'kishan' bhagat hai baba tera deevana

ujjain ke raja kabhi kirpa najariya dukhiya pe dalna re
ke raja kabhi kirpa najariya dukhiya pe dalna re
ujjain ke raja kabhi kirpa najariya dukhiya pe dalna re -2
raja mahaaraja kabhi kirpa najariya dukhiya pe dalna re

Vinod Kumar

UJJAIN KE RAJA BABA

dha	ge	n	ti	n	ke	dhi	n	dha	ge	n	ti	n	ke	dhi	n
1	2	3	4	5	6	7	8	1	2	3	4	5	6	7	8

S'S'R'　　M'M'　　P'　M'M'　R'　　R'R'　　S'R'　NR'S'　　S'
akaal　　mrityu　　vo　mare　jo　　kaam　　kare chaandal ka

S'　S'N　DPPM　R'　R'R'R'　R'　R'R'R'　S'N　R'R'　R'S'　　S'
aur kaal　uska　　kya　bighade jo bhagat　　ho mahaakaal　ka

music:
S' M' G' R' S' N, N S' P M – 3
M S' S' N N D P M N P
M G' G' R' R' S' S' N R' S'

S'S'　S'　S'S'　R'S'　N S'　NDPDM　N N　　N S'G'R'　S'
ujjain ke raja kabhi kirpa　　najariya dukhiya pe dalna　re

G'　R'G'　　R'S'
o　　bhole　baba

G'R'S'NS'R'M'
o------------------

M' M'　M' M'M' M'M'　M'G'P'　M'R'G'G'S'
ujjain　ke　raja kabhi　kirpa　najariya

G' G'　　G'　G'-NR'　G'R'S'
dukhiya pe　dalna　　re----

S'S'　S'　S'S'　　R'S'　N S'　NDPDM　N N　　N S'-G'R'　S'
raja mahaaraja kabhi kirpa　najariya　dukhiya pe dalna　　re

G'　R'G'　　R'S'
o　　bhole　baba

music:
M S'S'　S'R'G' R'S' N-G' R'S'- NPM -3
S'R'M'　M'M' M'M' P'M'G'R' S'N G'R'S' NPM
M S'S'　S'R'G' R'S' N-G' R'S'- R'G'M'-

M'M'M'M'   M'M'   M'G'P'   M'   R'-G'S'
parvati   pati shiv ji   hain   pyare

G'G'G'   R'R'   S'N   S'R'   R'S'S'   NN   S'R'   R'S'S'
kailash par   mere bhole viraje, mere bhole viraje

S'S'S'S'S'   R'S'   N   S'   NDPDM
mankaameshvar baba man ki muraadein

S'S'S'S'S'   R'S'   N   S'   NDPDM   N N   N   S'G'R'   S'
mahaaleshvar baba man ki muradein jholi me dalna   re

G'   R'G'   R'S'
o   bhole   baba

S'S'   S'   S'S'   R'S'   N S'   NDPDM   N N   N   S'G'R'   S'
ujjain ke raja kabhi   kirpa najariya dukhiya pe dalna re

M'M'   M'   M'M'   M'G'P'   M'   R'--G'S'
naino me jwala   aankhon   me jwala

G'G'   G'   R'S'N   S'R'   R'S'S'   NN   S'R'   R'S'S'
jata me ganga pahne mrigchhala bhole pahne mrigchhala

S'S'   S'   S'S'   R'S'   NNS'N   DPDM   N N   N   S'G'R'   S'
khulti hai jab unki tisri   vo ankhiyan-2 tandav kar dalna   re

S'S'   S'   S'S'   R'S'   N S'   NDPDM   N N   N   S'G'R'   S'
ujjain ke raja kabhi kirpa   najariya dukhiya pe dalna   re

G'M'   M'   M'M'   M'G'   P'   M'   R'G'G'S'
peete hain pyae bhar bhar ke bhangiya

G'G'G'   R'R'   S'N   S'   R'S'   S'S'   NN   S'   R'S'   S'S'S'
lagaaye dam bhole din aur ratiyaan, bhole din aur ratiyaan

S'S'   S'   S'S'   R'   S'   NNS'   NDPDM
baba tera bhagat hun main bahut deevana

S'S'   S'S'   S'   R'S'   N S'   NDPDM
'kishan' bhagat hai baba tera deevana

Vinod Kumar

N N N S'G'R' S'
kirpa kar dalna re

S'S' S' S'S' R'S' N S' NDPDM N N N S'G'R' S'
ujjain ke raja kabhi kirpa najariya   dukhiya pe dalna re -3

S'S' S' S'S'   R'S' N S' NDPDM N N N S'G'R' S'
raja mahaaraja kabhi kirpa najariya dukhiya pe dalna re

S'R' S'   S'S'   NN   S'R' S' S'S'S'
pite hain bhngiya bhole pite hain bhngiya

S'S'   S'R'   S' S'S'   S' N NS'   S'R' S'
akal   mrityu vo mare jo kam kare chndal ka

M'M'   M'M' M' M'M' M' R'   R'G' G'M' M'
akaal   mrityu vo mare jo kaam kare chaandal ka

M' M'M' M'M' G' G'G'G'   S' NN S' S'-R'S'   S'
aur kaal uska kya   bighade jo bhagat ho mahaakaal ka

S'S'S' S'S' R'S' S' S' S' S' NN R'S' S'
irade   roz bante hain aur ban kar tuut jate hain

M'M'M' M'M' M'M' M' M' M' M' R'R' G'G' M'
irade   roz   bante hain aur ban kar tuut jate hain

M'M' M'M' G'G' G' S'N   NS' S'R'S' S'
vahi ujjain jate hain jinhe baba bulate hain

S'N   NS'   S'R'S' S'
mere baba bulate hain

S'R' S'S' S' S' S'S' S' N NS' R' S'
karta kare n kar sake jo shiv kare so hoy

G'M'   M'M' M' M' M'M' M' R' R'G' G' M'
karta   kare n kar sake jo shiv kare so hoy

M' M' M'   M' G' G' G'G' NN R'R' R' S'
aur tiin lok me shiv ke jaisa duja koyi n hoy

```
NN   R'R'   R'   S'   NN      NN   R'R'   R'   S'
duja koii    n  hoy bhole   duja koyii   n  hoy

S'S'   S'  S'S'   R'S'   N S'   NDPDM      N N    N S'G'R'  S'
ujjain ke raja kabhi kirpa najariya-, dukhiya pe dalna re -2
```

34. YE JAGAT BADA DUKHDAYI

Bhajan
Lyrics: Pujya Sri Rajesh Ji
Taal: Kaharwa
Singer: Pujya Sri Rajeshwaranand Ji Maharaj
Chord: SGP GPN   S=C#
https://youtu.be/foimuUZUGUc

parchhayi bhi hoti paraayi sukh ki aas tajo mere bhaii
ye jagat badaa dukhdayi, sukh ki aas tajo mere bhaii

usne hi dukh paya sukh ki aasha rakkhi jisne
is duniya se moh badhakar bolo pyare kisne
kab chain ki bansi bajaaii, sukh ki aas tajo mere bhaii

jisko tumne apna samjhaa nikla vahi paraaya
tere huye n koii lekin tujhko hosh na aaya
kaii bar hai thokar khaii, sukh ki aas tajo mere bhaii

duniya dikhti nayi hai lekin khel purane chalte
dohrata itihaas swayam ko kewal paatr badalte
bas riiti yahi chali aayii, sukh ki aas tajo mere bhaii

hota kabhi mahabharat kabhi banti hai ramayan
kabhi kans kabhi raavan ke hit aate hain narayan
kabhi krishna kabhi rahuraaii, sukh ki aas tajo mere bhaii

jag se sukh ki aasha tajkar ram bharose rah le
man ko manmohan ka banaakar 'rajesh' mukh se kah le
sri ram sharan sukhdayi, sukh ki aas tajo mere bhaii
ye jagat badaa dukhdaayi, sukh ki aas tajo mere bhaii

Vinod Kumar

YE JAGAT BADA DUKHDAYI

dha	ge	n	ti	n	ke	dhi	n	dha	ge	n	ti	n	ke	dhi	n
1	2	3	4	5	6	7	8	1	2	3	4	5	6	7	8
														S'	S'
														p	r
-	-	N	-	-	S'	-	S'	S'	-	-	-	-	D	-	P
-	-	chha	-	-	yi	-	bhi	ho	-	-	-	-	ti	-	p
D	-	-	-	M	-	G	-	-	-	P	D	-	P	M	-
ra	-	-	-	yi	-	-	-	-	-	su	kh	-	ki	-	-
G	-	G	-	-	M	-	P	M	-	-	-	-	G	-	R
-	-	aa	-	-	s	-	t	jo	-	-	-	-	me	-	re
S	-	-	-	S	-	-	-	-	-	-	-	S'	-	-	-
bha	-	-	-	ii	-	-	-	-	-	-	-	ye	-	-	-
-	-	N	N	-	S'	-	R'	S'	-	-	-	-	D	-	P
-	-	j	g	-	t	-	b	da	-	-	-	-	du	-	kh
D	-	-	-	M	-	G	-	-	-	P	D	-	P	M	-
da	-	-	-	yi	-	-	-	-	-	su	kh	-	ki	-	-
G	-	G	-	-	M	-	P	M	-	-	-	-	G	-	R
-	-	aa	-	-	s	-	t	jo	-	-	-	-	me	-	re
S	-	-	-	S	-	-	-	-	-						
bha	-	-	-	ii	-	-	-	-	-						
P	P	P	-	M	-	G	M	M	P	P	-	P	P	P	-
u	s	ne	-	hi	-	du	kh	pa	-	ya	-	su	kh	ki	-
N	-	N	-	N	-	D	-	P	P	P	-	-	-	-	-
aa	-	sha	-	r	k	khi	-	ji	s	ne	-	-	-	-	-
P	P	P	P	M	-	G	M	P	-	P	P	P	-	P	P
i	s	du	ni	or	-	se	-	mo	-	h	b	dha	-	k	r
N	-	N	-	N	-	D	-	P	P	P	-	-	-	S'	S'
bo	-	lo	-	pya	-	re	-	ki	s	ne	-	-	-	k	b

```
N    -    -    -  | -    S'   -    R' | S'   -    -    -  | -    D    -    P
chai -    -    -  | -    n    -    ki | bn   -    -    -  | -    si   -    b

D    -    -    -  | M    -    G    -  | -    -    P    D  | -    P    M    -
ja   -    -    -  | yi   -    -    -  | -    -    su   kh | -    ki   -    -

G    -    G    -  | -    M    -    P  | M    -    -    -  | -    G    -    R
-    -    aa   -  | -    s    -    t  | jo   -    -    -  | -    me   -    re

S    -    -    -  | S    -    -    -  | -    -
bha  -    -    -  | ii   -    -    -  | -    -


P    P    P    -  | M    -    G    M  | M    P    P    -  | P    P    P    -
ji   s    ko   -  | tu   m    ne   -  | a    p    na   -  | s    m    jha  -

D    N    N    -  | D    N    -    D  | P    -    P    -  | -    -    -    -
ni   k    la   -  | v    hi   -    p  | ra   -    ya   -  | -    -    -    -

P    -    P    -  | M    G    -    M  | M    -    P    -  | P    -    P    -
te   -    re   -  | hu   e    -    n  | ko   -    ii   -  | le   -    ki   n

N    N    N    -  | N    -    D    D  | P    -    P    -  | -    -    S'   S'
tu   jh   ko   -  | ho   -    sh   n  | aa   -    ya   -  | -    -    k    ii

N    -    -    -  | -    S'   -    R' | S'   -    -    -  | -    D    -    P
ba   -    -    -  | -    r    -    hai| tho  -    -    -  | -    k    -    r

D    -    -    -  | M    -    G    -  | -    -    P    D  | -    P    M    -
kha  -    -    -  | ii   -    -    -  | -    -    su   kh | -    ki   -    -

G    -    G    -  | -    M    -    P  | M    -    -    -  | -    G    -    R
-    -    aa   -  | -    s    -    t  | jo   -    -    -  | -    me   -    re

S    -    -    -  | S    -    -    -  | -    -    -    -  | -    -    -    -
bha  -    -    -  | ii   -    -    -  | -    -    -    -  | -    -    -    -

P    P    P    -  | M    M    G    M  | M    P    -    P  | P    -    P    P
du   ni   ya   -  | di   kh   ti   -  | n    yi   -    hai| le   -    ki   n
```

Vinod Kumar

N	-	N	N	N	-	D	-	P	P	P	-	-	-	-	-
khe	-	l	pu	ra	-	ne	-	ch	l	te	-	-	-	-	re

P	P	P	-	M	-	G	M	P	-	P	P	P	-	P	-
do	h	ra	-	ta	-	i	ti	ha	-	s	sw	ym	-	ko	-

N	-	N	-	N	-	D	D	P	P	P	-	S'	-	S'	-
ke	-	v	l	pa	-	tr	b	d	l	te	-	b	-	s	-

N	-	-	-	-	S'	-	R'	S'	-	-	-	-	D	P	-
ri	-	-	-	-	ti	-	y	hi	-	-	-	-	ch	li	-

D	-	-	-	M	-	G	-	-	-	P	D	-	P	M	-
aa	-	-	-	yi	-	-	-	-	-	su	kh	-	ki	-	-

G	-	G	-	-	M	-	P	M	-	-	-	-	G	-	R
-	-	aa	-	-	s	-	t	jo	-	-	-	-	me	-	re

S	-	-	-	S	-	-	-	-	-	-	-				
bha	-	-	-	ii	-	-	-	-	-	-	-				

P	-	P	-	M	M	G	M	P	-	P	-	P	P	P	P
ho	-	ta	-	k	bhi	-	m	ha	-	bha	-	r	t	k	bhi

N	-	N	-	N	-	D	-	P	-	P	-	-	-	-	-
b	n	ti	-	hai	-	ra	-	ma	-	y	n	-	-	-	-

P	P	-	P	-	M	G	M	P	-	P	P	P	-	P	P
k	bhi	-	kn	-	s	k	bhi	ra	-	v	n	ke	-	hi	t

N	-	N	-	N	-	D	-	P	-	P	P	-	-	S'	S'
aa	-	te	-	hain	-	na	-	ra	-	y	n	-	-	k	bhi

N	-	-	-	-	S'	-	R'	S'	-	-	-	-	D	-	P
kri	-	-	-	-	shna	-	k	bhi	-	-	-	-	r	-	ghu

D	-	-	-	M	-	G	-	-	-	P	D	-	P	M	-
ra	-	-	-	yi	-	-	-	-	-	su	kh	-	ki	-	-

G	-	G	-	-	M	-	P	M	-	-	-	-	G	-	R
-	-	aa	-	-	s	-	t	jo	-	-	-	-	me	-	re

S	-	-	-	S	-	-	-	-	-						
bha	-	-	-	ii	-	-	-	-	-						
P	P	P	-	M	M	<u>G</u>	M	M	P	P	-	P	P	P	-
j	g	se	-	su	kh	ki	-	aa	-	sha	-	t	j	k	r
<u>N</u>	-	<u>N</u>	<u>N</u>	<u>N</u>	-	<u>D</u>	-	P	P	P	-	-	-	-	-
ra	-	m	bh	ro	-	se	-	r	h	le	-	-	-	-	-
P	P	P	-	M	M	<u>G</u>	M	M	P	P	P	P	-	P	-
m	n	ko	-	m	n	mo	-	h	n	ka	b	na	-	k	r
<u>N</u>	-	<u>N</u>	<u>N</u>	<u>N</u>	<u>D</u>	<u>D</u>	-	P	P	P	-	-	-	S'	-
ra	-	je	sh	mu	kh	se	-	k	h	le	-	-	-	sri	-
N	-	-	-	-	S'	-	R'	S'	-	S'	-	-	<u>D</u>	-	P
ra	-	-	-	-	m	-	sh	r	-	n	-	-	su	-	kh
<u>D</u>	-	-	-	M	-	<u>G</u>	-	-	-	P	<u>D</u>	-	P	M	-
da	-	-	-	yi	-	-	-	-	-	su	kh	-	ki	-	-
<u>G</u>	-	<u>G</u>	-	-	M	-	P	M	-	-	-	-	<u>G</u>	-	<u>R</u>
-	-	aa	-	-	s	-	t	jo	-	-	-	-	me	-	re
S	-	-	-	S	-	-	-	-	-						
bha	-	-	-	ii	-	-	-	-	-						

36. SARGAM OR ALANKAR OR PALTE

S R G M P D N S'
S' N D P M G R S

SS RR GG MM PP DD NN S'S'
S'S' NN DD PP MM GG RR SS

SSS RRR GGG MMM PPP DDD NNN S'S'S'
S'S'S' NNN DDD PPP MMM GGG RRR SSS

SR RG GM MP PD DN NS'
S'N ND DP PM MG GR RS

SRG- RGM- GMP- MPD PDN- DNS'-
S'ND- NDP- DPM- PMG- MGR- GRS-

SRGM RGMP GMPD MPDN PDNS'
S'NDP NDPM DPMG PMGR MGRS

SRGMP RGMPD GMPDN MPDNS'
S'NDPM NDPMG DPMGR PMGRS

SG RM GP MD PN DS'
S'D NP DM PG MR GS

SM RP GD MN PS'
S'P NM DG PR MS

SP RD GN MS'
S'M NG DR PS

SD RN GS'
S'G NR DS

SRSRG– RGRGM– GMGMP- MPMPD– PDPDN– DNDNS'-
S'NS'ND- NDNDP– DPDPM– PMPMG–MGMGR– GRGRS-

SRGSRSRG RGMRGRGM GMPGMGMP
MPDMPMP PDNPDPD DNS'DNDNS'

S'NDS'NS'ND NDPNDNDP DPMDPDPM
PMGPMPMG MGMGMGR GRSGRGRS
S
S R S
S R G R S
S R G M G R S
S R G M P M G R S
S R G M P D P M G R S
S R G M P D N D P M G R S
S R G M P D N S' S' N D P M G R S

S'
S' N S'
S' N D N S'
S' N D P D N S'
S' N D P M P D N S'
S' N D P M G M P D N S'
S' N D P M G R G M P D N S'
S' N D P M G R S R G M P D N S'

S-SRG- R-RGM- G-GMP- M-MPD- P-PDN- D-DNS'-
S'-S'ND- N-NDP- D-DPM- P-PMG- M-MGR- G-GRS-
RS GR MG PM DP ND S'N R'S'
NS' DN PD MP GM RG SR .NS

SGR RMG GPM MDP PND DS'N NR'S'
S'DN NPD DMP PGM MRG GSR R.NS

.P P .DD .NN SS' RR' GG' MM'
M'M G'G R'R S'S N.N D.D P.P

Vinod Kumar

Raag: Bhairav
S R̲ G M P D̲ N S'
S' N D̲ P M G R̲ S

Raag: Bhairavi
S R̲ G̲ M P D̲ N̲ S'
S' N̲ D̲ P M G̲ R̲ S

Raag: Aasavari
S R G̲ M P D̲ N̲ S'
S' N̲ D̲ P M G̲ R S

Raag: Malkauns
S G̲ M D̲ N̲ S'
S' N̲ D̲ M G̲ S

37. OTHER BOOKS OF VINOD KUMAR

"Mukesh 51 Songs' Sargam" Part 1, 2,

"Lata 51 Songs' Sargam"

"Kishore 51 Songs' Sargam" Part 1, 2

"Md. Rafi 51 Songs' Sargam" Part 1, 2, 3, 4

"Asha 51 Songs' Sargam" Part 1

"S D Burman and Yesudas 51 Songs' Sargam"

"Manna Dey 51 Songs' Sargam"

"Composer S D Burman 51 Songs' Sargam"

"Superhit 51 Gazals Sargam"

"Kumar Shanu 51 Songs' Sargam"

"Bhajan Swarlipi" Part 1, 2, 3, 4

"Suman Kalyanpur 51 Songs' Sargam"

"Sabad and Punjabi Songs Sargam" Part 1

 "Sloan duployan shorthand book"

"Mahendra Kapoor 51 Songs' Sargam"

These Books are available in English SRGM and Western CDEFG style at notionpress.com , amazon.in , indiamart.com and at Flipkart.com

For English SRGM books search... (Singer name) 51 Songs' Sargam, book.

For Western CDEFG books search... (Singer name) Songs' Western Notes, book.

If you like the book pl. tell others. If any suggestion pl. mail me. Vinod Kumar (vinod66vk@gmail.com)

Vinod Kumar

Vinod Kumar की 51 गीतों की सरगम पुस्तकें flipkart.com से खरीदने हेतु, अपने मोबाईल से नीचे दिए क्यू आर कोड को स्कैन करें. (Hindi, English, Western all)

Vinod Kumar की 51 गीतों की सरगम पुस्तकें amazon.in से खरीदने हेतु, अपने मोबाईल से नीचे दिए क्यू आर कोड को स्कैन करें. (Hindi, English, Western all)

अधिक जानकारी हेतु संपर्क करें
kavitaprakashan7@gmail.com
किताबों को खरीदने हेतु संपर्क करें.
mob:**9452904656**
ये पुस्तकें किसी शॉप पर नहीं मिलेगी